All the Fish Are Butterflies

A Memoir by

Joan Marie

ISBN: 979-8-9880272-0-1

Out & About Town Press, 7200 13th Street North,

St. Petersburg, FL 33702. Email: angelusmichael@ymail.com

Drawings in the memoir are by Joan Marie

This memoir is dedicated to all
who are affected by mental illness.

I thank my wonderful children, Lori and Michael, for providing love and emotional support.

THE MERMAID'S SONG

Warm is the sun on the quick-silver sea,
white and translucent as my soul.
Once in the days of faraway—all gone,
when the tide was high beneath the new moon.

I was born in the pale-grey sandcastle
that once was my grandmother's home,
my hair thick with seaweed
awaiting the first sundrop.

Now my hair flows freely on the rising tide,
for I am blonde!
I am blonde!
And all the fish are butterflies
in my sea of sun.
I have touched their rainbowed wings
brimming with little yellow suns,
and aquamarine eyes.

Blue being the color of my heart
while the sea and I are one.
My curves trickle turquoise sequins,
as I sing my siren's song.

While playing, on my blushing harp
beneath a starfish sky,
The Song of the Sequined Sailor
in the sea of time—
"You are mine,
you are mine."

Am I not the Lorelei?
While all the sea sighs—
"You are mine,
you are mine,"
and all the fish are butterflies.

John Corcione

It's those forever places in our mind—an old house, a bench beside the sea, or a stretch of beach—that remind us of people who once were a part of our lives. This is the story of the people in my life and how I remember them.

1

The year was 1961, and I was a fair-haired girl in a golden world. I lived in a stately home in an upscale neighborhood on the Jersey Shore and was a member of a well-respected family. My parents appeared to be happily married, and my father was a successful businessman. They were the good times—Asbury Park's glory days. My mother was well then. It was only a year before the scream in the night. My family was oblivious to the demon lurking in the dark recesses of our home.

The beast sat outside a window, crouching like a wide-eyed gargoyle, baring its horrid teeth, waiting to slink through a crevice in the wall and destroy our unsuspecting family. That double demon didn't destroy my family all at once, that would have been too easy. It infiltrated our sanctuary and destroyed us slowly, like water falling, drop by drop, on the face of a stone. It lived in Pandemonium, that noisy hall of demons. I have met that demon face to face; it is legion. Its name is mental illness.

My mother's breakdown was the beginning of sorrows. As a rule, one cannot blame all their problems on their parents. It is difficult to admit this, but I, too, have joined the ranks of mothers who made stupid mistakes. I, too, have been guilty of the same stupidity. I tried desperately to avoid my mother's mistakes and my mother's illness. I was true to my promise. I never made the same mistakes as my mother. I am original: I made my own.

I wanted to be remembered as a good, faithful wife and mother, but sometimes I think I failed. One thing, I was passionate about life and relationships. Material possessions didn't interest me. I loved wildly and not too well. I loved my husband. I hated my husband. I loved my kids dearly, but sometimes I wished I hadn't brought them into my troubled world. No matter how hard I tried, my life was a spiral of downward mobility. You could say I went from riches to rags. I grew up in a time of stay-at-home moms and the good-natured girl next door.

Like any little girl, one of my favorite pastimes was sneaking into my mother's room and parading about in her clothes. Pearl necklaces and rhinestone earrings rested quietly in their black velvet hideaway, waiting for me to adorn my small neck. I clumped around the hardwood floors like a chorus girl. I sashayed over to my mother's dressing table and gingerly picked up her favorite lipstick. I tried to draw a simple cupid's bow on my lips, but the lipstick made me look like the Riddler. Regardless, I thought I looked stunning.

In a few years I would emerge from my chrysalis as a butterfly, waiting for my delicate wings to dry. My transformation from tomboy to teen wasn't easy, but I always had a special person I could turn to—my grandmother. Gran was my mother's mother, and matriarch of the family. Since my mother addressed Gran as "Mother," I called my mother "Mother," too. My grandmother was an aristocratic woman of wisdom if not misfortune.

In summer, I stayed with Gran at her modest home in Bradley Beach. In winter, Gran lived at our home in Interlaken. Grandparents weren't shuttered away in assisted-living facilities. There were no gated communities or retirement villages in those days. Grandparents were a stabilizing influence and an integral part of the family.

Gran lived a life of secrets. People down at the shore called her a "blue-nosed Methodist." She was born in 1886, some twenty years after the end of the Civil War. Her parents provided her with a private tutor and piano lessons when she was young. Gran was highly educated for a woman of her time. One of her favorite quotes was, "Backward, turn backward, O time in thy flight, make me a child again just for tonight."

It took me a lifetime to appreciate the significance of that quote, but now I understand Gran's longing. If only *I* could go back in time and shake off the tragedies that haunt me. If only I could wipe out the struggles, the sickness, and the trauma, I would transform my life and the lives of my loved ones forever. Unfortunately, the hands of time are not kind—they're made of steel. Try as we can, we cannot turn them back. Life isn't a movie set where we can travel "Back to the Future." We can't erect, stage, and dismantle our own movie sets at will.

Whenever I face adversity, I pray that I can rise to the occasion. Maybe I'm not the queen of steel, but I must not allow myself, as Sylvia Plath wrote, to "break to the beaks of birds." I shudder at the vision of a bleeding, dying creature surrounded by hovering, flapping vultures. I must ascend, silence the cacophony, and drive the vultures away.

I longed to be a child again, to run free in the woods, to climb trees, and listen to the wind whisper through the pines. The people I loved will be there, but this time I'll rewrite the script. There will be no catastrophes.

It would be autumn and the leaves are just starting to fall. I can hear the *ping* of gravel as my father's sleek black Chrysler rolls up the driveway, scattering pebbles against the rimmed whitewalls and crunching the bright leaves beneath the wheels. I am sitting on the wobbly swing set, and my little brothers are playing catch under the old backyard oak. Pot roast is bubbling on the stove.

My mother opens the screen door and calls to us, "Let's go! Dinner's ready. Your father's home."

We tumble into the dining room, and Gran ushers us into our seats at the big table. We gobble up our food so we can all watch TV together.

September at the Jersey Shore was soothing, but the summers were magical. I splashed in the ocean and rode the waves until I was exhausted, then dozed on the beach until my skin turned bronze in the summer sun. The brilliant globe would burn away into the west, then I would trudge upstairs in my grandmother's house and curl up in her sturdy four-poster bed like a little fawn.

The 1950s was a decade of domesticity. My mother, like many women, tried to be the perfect wife. Thirteen years younger than my father, she encouraged him to take dance lessons and play golf. My father disliked golf and country clubs, but he loved music and was a good dancer. On Thursday nights, I would lean over the banister, listening to the rhythmic beat of the rumba as it glided up the stairs and mingled with my parent's laughter.

It was a good time to be blonde. Television was a new and exciting medium. Even though our TV received only three channels, we were spellbound by this new entertainment. The Lone Ranger and Roy Rogers were popular cowboys, "Father Knows Best" and "Our Gang Comedies" were popular family fare. Young boys looked up to baseball stars such as Joe DiMaggio and Mickey Mantle. Every Saturday morning, my younger brother George and I went to the St. James Theater to watch serials and cowboy movies. I wonder how much those early movies inspired Asbury natives Danny

DeVito and Vic Morrow to become actors. Mike, my future husband, even claimed to have had a fight with Jack Nicholson, who lived in neighboring Neptune City, and confessed that Jack won.

The world has changed drastically since I was seventeen. The 1960's, exciting and prosperous at first, became years of upheaval and rebellion. The Civil Rights and Women's Movements would change society forever. Traditions were trampled down and society spun out of control.

Like many teenagers, I thought my parents were oppressive and old-fashioned. I admit that I was a self-centered twit. In *The Great Gatsby,* Daisy advises her daughter to be "a silly, pretty, little fool." I took Daisy's advice. I was sixteen and my life revolved around socializing and being popular. Life was just too exciting to spend time working in my family's candy store. I could hardly wait to break free of my family, school, and work.

There was an exciting world outside my dull little town. I dreamed of hopping on a train, running away, and never coming back.

My family and I lived in the small town of Interlaken, which lies hidden between another small town, Allenhurst, and much larger Asbury Park. Nestled between two lakes, it is named after Interlaken, a small town in Switzerland that is situated between Lake Brienz and Lake Reines, just below Switzerland's Itger Mountains. It is an idyllic pastoral town complete with rustic retreats, flower-laden streets, and breathtaking mountain vistas. Maybe my hometown didn't offer spectacular mountain views, but it did offer elegant homes and stately oaks.

You better slow down if you drive through my old hometown. The speed limit is 20 MPH and strictly enforced. Brick pillars still grace the entrance to this unique town, while flashing red lights and black and white crossing gates guard the railroad tracks to my old hometown.

The crossing gates were only three blocks from my home. Any time of day or night, you could hear the trains whistling and chugging along the rails. The cars lumbered along, dropping off businessmen and travelers at the Allenhurst station. Bells clanged, red lights flashed, and the gates dropped, signaling the cars and pedestrians to stop and stand clear. The engineer sounded three long whistles, and the steel wheels clicked wildly as the cars whirled by, spinning golden images like a magic lantern. The locomotive plowed along, grating against the steel rails and rattling down the narrow track. The train picked up steam as it slid down the creosote rails, south toward Asbury Park. Dust flew behind the red caboose, as it raced its shadow in the muddy lake below. Someday, I thought, I would hop on that train and run away to a new place and leave my hometown forever.

You know the saying: "Be careful what you wish for."

Sometimes late at night, the "Owl Train" would interrupt my dreams, rousing me from deep sleep. The sound of thundering wheels rumbled through my bedroom like a charging bull, roaring and chugging fearfully, shattering the night stillness. Science calls this phenomenon the Doppler effect, but to me the whistle blast was the call of the wild. I was afraid that my soul would take flight and I would have to wake up and frantically clasp it back to my body. I would toss and turn, pulling the thick covers over my head, trying to fall back asleep.

Most of the time, the sound of the train was soothing. I loved the sound of the rattle-clack-clack of the wheels and the promise of faraway. Trains bring back memories. Sometimes they remind me of Gregory and Dennis, my childhood neighbors. Every Christmas, they lugged their built-to-scale railroad up from the cellar and assembled a mini-village along the sun porch of their Dutch Colonial home. The village was a working microcosm of life. Mechanical cattle cars shuttled tiny steers onto a ramp while minute milk cans sat on a narrow platform. Drab freight cars waited patiently as black cranes hoisted toy logs onto the waiting flatbed. Blinking red lights signaled the approaching train as white smoke puffed from the black locomotive. The entire village was carpeted in fake snow.

Miniature models of children lined up outside the red-brick schoolhouse as the little yellow school bus rounded the corner. Businessmen stood at the station, waiting for the train to transport them home. In the center of town stood a simple white church, its snowy windows all lit up for Christmas. A green wreath decorated the bakery door, a sign in the window announced *"Fresh Gingerbread."* Gregory would flip a switch and the tiny houses would light up as the trains chugged around the track.

It was a perfect Christmas in a perfect little town, in a perfect little world. If only we all could live in such a perfect world. Unfortunately, it was a world that existed only in Christmas villages. It was a world that my mother tried to recreate, and almost succeeded.

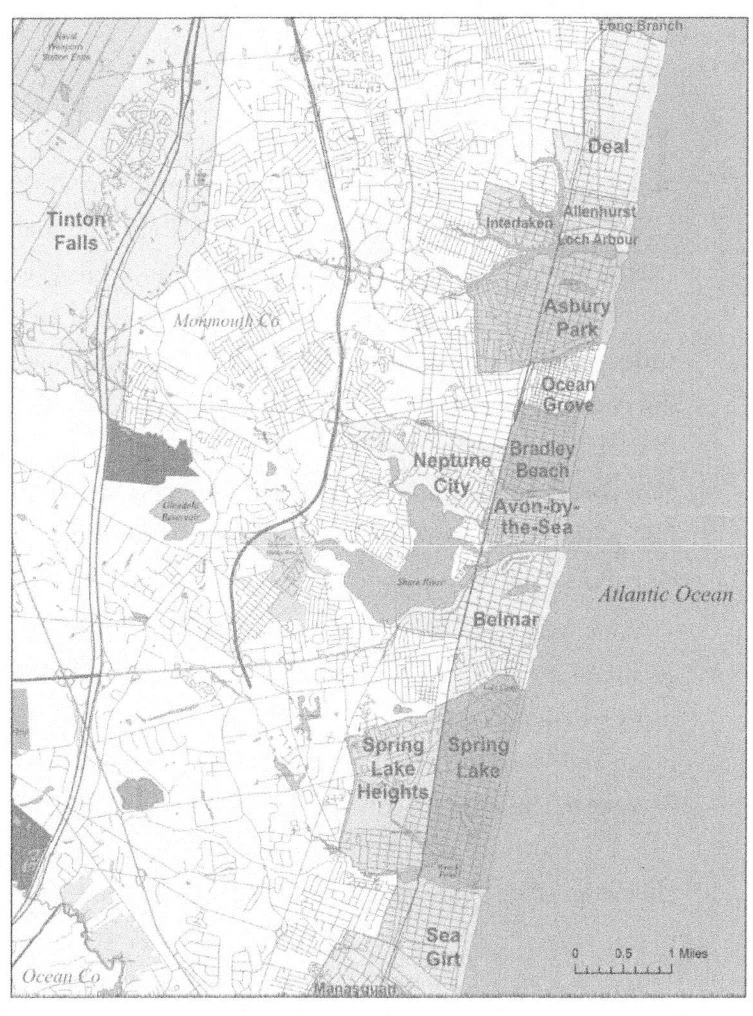

The Jersey Shore—Asbury Park and neighboring towns

2

In 1921, babies were traditionally born at home. The local doctor carried a black satchel and made house visits. My mother was born on Christmas day in a sleepy Victorian town called Ocean Grove, a small bed and breakfast municipality complete with Queen Anne homes, local antiques, and narrow horse-and-buggy streets. One cottage still had its original hitching post. The homes stood shoulder-to-shoulder to one another, their round turrets and gingerbread trim competing for attention. The Methodist Camp Meeting Association founded Ocean Grove after the end of the Civil War.

American flags waved in the breeze and bright red geraniums tumbled out of white window boxes. In the 1900s, many vacationers journeyed from Philadelphia to enjoy the beach and worship at the Ocean Grove Great Auditorium. Every year, choir groups converged at the Great Auditorium to raise their voices in song. On summer nights, the strains of old hymns echoed through the timbered walls and glided out to sea.

My grandmother's family vacationed in Ocean Grove in the summer. I idolized my adventurous cousins, Ricky, Robert, and Billy. During those endless summers, they taught me how to catch killifish and ride the waves. My mother's family reminded me of Swiss Family Robinson. I visualized them gripping the wheel of a Dutch clipper ship through a fierce nor'easter, only to be shipwrecked on a desert island. I imagined the boys whittling bamboo fishing poles and snagging tarpon in the blue waters. Before long, the boys would lash palm fronds together and sail into the sunset while my father's family opened a diner on the beach.

My grandmother, Aimee, was as stoic as a statue. She was slender, blue-eyed, and as silent as the Sphinx. In fact, she kept more secrets than the Sphinx. Gran had the patriotism of George Washington. In fact, with her white hair and aquiline nose, she *resembled* George Washington.

I only saw her cry once when I was eighteen. That was the day she told me the truth about my grandfather. It was the day that helped me to understand some of the reasons for my mother's nervous breakdown. When I think of my family's deception, I'm furious.

Mother's family was so poor that my Uncle Wilbur had to quit school and work on the fishing boats to feed the family. Winter whiting was a family staple. In summer, Wilbur brought home enough flounder, bluefish, and bonito to feed the family. Uncle Bobby worked at the local produce store and brought home leftover produce.

Gran's family had left the oppressive heat of Philadelphia to spend their summers at the Jersey Shore. Inevitably, my grandmother had fallen for a handsome lifeguard. He was a swimmer and a volunteer fireman, and he must have cut a dashing figure to a sheltered girl from Philadelphia. Gran described him racing his team of white horses through the narrow streets, careening the red fire wagon past throngs of frenzied onlookers as he rushed toward the flames.

Gran's family disowned her. She had married beneath her. There was nothing for her to do but forget her privileged life in Philadelphia and embrace the Jersey Shore.

* * *

Mother, having been born on Christmas Day, loved Christmas and decorated the house with big red bows, fresh greens, and holly. I remember the scent of pine garlands on the mantle, while a fire, crackling in the red-brick fireplace, spit yellow sparks against the black-mesh screen. Mother once created a gingerbread house dripping with frosty white icing, candy canes, and multicolored gumdrops.

My mother's name was Marjorie, Marjorie Elizabeth Vanderslice. Marjorie was the granddaughter of the Main Line Millers of Philadelphia, and her grandfather was an importer. My grandmother's antique silver tea set linked her ancestral lineage to royalty. Before I was born, this treasured heirloom dignified my grandmother's mahogany sideboard. Gran passed it down to my mother as a wedding gift. The tea set boasted a miniature bust of Queen Victoria perched hawk-like atop the coffee server. Mother polished the set until it shone like a minted coin. When my mother got sick, she sprayed her heirloom silver and never polished the set again. This may have been the beginning of her liberation.

My mother was a natural beauty. Her appearance was the core of her being. Whenever she walked down Cookman Avenue, a fashionable street in Asbury Park, people would stop, stare, and smile. Her crisp Nordic features, champagne-blonde hair, and shapely figure mesmerized. She preferred expensive, fashionably tailored clothes. Many years later, I was surprised to discover that she grew up in poverty.

I could try to describe my mother, but only a photograph can do her justice. Sometimes she wore her thick hair in an upsweep or styled the long strands into a soft pageboy.

As glamorous as she was, the beach was my mother's salvation. Maybe her undoing. Mother would dab her lips with "Cyclamen Evening" lipstick, sweep her eyelids with pastel-blue eye shadow, and head for the beach. Loch Arbour, her favorite beach, was only a ten-minute drive away. Mother could drop what she was doing, slap some tuna-fish sandwiches together, pack us kids into the car, and head for the beach. We would drive through the gate, unpack the car, and set up camp.

It never failed, just as we were setting up the beach umbrella, Mother would turn and say, "Well, did you children know that when I was young, I was voted Miss Bradley Beach?"

"Yes, we know," we sighed.

"Captain of the Asbury swim team, too!" she beamed.

Once we were settled, my mother would study the sea for the wind and the tide.

"It's a perfect beach day! No wind, tide's coming in," she announced, searching her beach bag for her bathing cap. She was a great swimmer.

It was a family transgression not to go in the water unless you had a good excuse. We were trained to stand by the shore until the wavelets washed over our ankles and numbed our legs. Only then could we wade into the icy Atlantic.

Mother would calmly walk toward the sea, test the water, and immerse herself in the sea, ignoring the idle beachgoers who lounged about on beach chairs.

There was an incident at the Allenhurst beach when I was in my early teens. My mother was wading in the water, two boys were throwing rocks on the beach, and a random stone hit my mother in the back of her head. I remember running alongside the ambulance attendants as they carried her away on a stretcher. She was taken to the local hospital and never did seem right after that. I always wondered about that head injury.

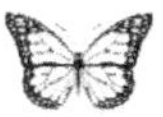

3

A beautiful woman likes to surround herself with beautiful things, and my mother was no exception. Mother insisted that "purple is the color of royalty." Visitors puzzled over the purple velvet sofa that reigned over the living room, and the purple paisley wallpaper that graced the master bedroom and bath. The dining room featured my mother's prized possession, a crystal teardrop chandelier. When the sun set, sunbeams swept prisms of light against the ceiling, flicking rainbows against the soft pink walls.

I think my mother was just being humorous when, years later, she whispered to me in all confidence: "I wish my chandelier could accompany me in my final resting place."

My mother was Holland Dutch, Pennsylvania Dutch, and English. My father was Greek. All my life I've been culturally confused. Mother tried desperately to be accepted by the Greeks, and the hard-working Greek community of Asbury Park embraced and welcomed her. My father's family did not, labeling my mother a "gold-digger." It just goes to show you how some people looked down on you if you came from poverty.

I didn't know that my mother grew up poor until after she became sick. Years later, Mother told me how, as a child, she sat shivering by an old coal stove. She wore used clothes and stuffed her shoes with toilet paper, causing her feet to be misshapen from ill-fitting shoes. Nevertheless, she blossomed like an orchid in a rainforest.

My mother was the direct opposite of the stereotypical dark eyed, black skirted Yia-Yia. If my father had wanted a Greek girl, he would have married one. Once, my father confided to me that he never really wanted to marry a Greek girl. Yet when Mother took lessons to learn the Greek language, her tutor commended her progress saying, "Margie, I think that way back, you must have been Greek."

My mother assembled a collection of cookbooks, stacking them up on the old radiator by the bay window until the pages curled up and yellowed from the heat. Mother liked to bake, and I often heard her laughing when she baked bread or layered phyllo dough. They were happy times then. Easter featured a holiday table laden with honeyed baklava, mounds of sugary *kourabiedes*, and syrupy *galakaboureko*. I still remember the aroma of honey and nuts floating through the house.

Even so, Mother always wondered what was wrong. Maybe society demanded too much of a beautiful woman. The other wives appeared relaxed and happy in their marriages. She wondered why other women seemed to have such security and contentment in their lives while she was forever striving for recognition. Trying to be a model wife and mother was difficult. There were just too many demands—too many people to please. Mother wondered why *her* husband always seemed to be preoccupied. The answer was simple. It would have been a fair fight if Mother could wage war against the sultry wiles of another woman, but my father's first love was no mere human, but a goddess of his own creation.

My father was a candy maker, a businessman and co-owner of a small candy store. The store was located on Cookman Avenue, just around the corner from Main Street, and a few blocks from the Asbury Park boardwalk. The Caramel Shop featured homemade chocolates, fudge, and caramels. My father's business was his life and his love, and he worked at the store almost every day. My mother's attempts to please him were mostly unsuccessful.

It's easy to look back on our parents' flaws and overlook our own parental imperfections. Each sibling views his or her childhood in a different perspective. Don't get me wrong, my father was a wonderful, charismatic man. Everybody loved him. Not a day goes by that I don't think of him. I can still visualize him sitting at the dining room table like a swarthy potentate, commanding his lamb and potatoes as though they were loyal subjects. My mother had prepared his favorite meal, but after dinner he tossed his napkin aside, ran his fingers through his black, wavy hair and announced: "Margie, I've got to get back to the store." Pushing his plate aside, he arose from the dinner table and slipped through the French doors, just as a stray mosquito buzzed through the open screen.

My mother stood there and sighed. She waved to him as he hopped into his car, revved the engine, and backed out of the driveway. As my father drove away, he nearly sideswiped a tree.

He didn't even kiss my mother goodbye. She closed the doors quietly and cleared the table, swatting the errant mosquito.

I guess Mother tolerated being second best for many years. Even as a young girl, I sensed that something was wrong. My mother was quiet and seldom raised her voice. That's why, years later, her sudden scream in the night was frightening. It was very uncharacteristic of my mother to scream like a banshee.

What was she screaming about? I'll never know, but the scream in the night was the beginning of the end, the beginning of a vicious illness that held my mother's mind hostage and temporarily darkened her soul. Slowly the disease descended until my mother was caught in a dangerous whirlpool, pulling her down, down, down, sweeping her away.

4

When I was young, I assumed that the candy store would be there forever. I thought my life would just go on and on, but today the old store has been replaced by an upscale artist's gallery. The loyal, hardworking candy makers and salesgirls are gone, too.

I remember standing by the storefront and leaning closer, pressing my nose against the window. I peered in. The store seemed much smaller than I had remembered. Slick hardwood floors and warm earth tones had replaced the original pale peach walls and sea-foam green linoleum. Contemporary paintings crowded the walls. Angular, distorted portraits were carefully arranged among colorful still life and floating Chagall imposters. I tried the door, but it was locked. There were no customers. The store was empty of humanity. The shiny glass candy counters had disappeared, but their rainbow streaks were etched in my memory. I visualized the customers touching the glass and pointing to their selections.

How I used to polish those cases—spritzing and wiping them until I could see my reflection. I was sixteen then. My profile seemed somewhat nondescript, a half-breed at best. Sometimes I would turn my face to the side, admiring my distorted profile in the glass. I knew I would never be as beautiful as my mother, but I had a good personality and all the sassiness of youth. No, not me, I would never grow old. I would pine away and die young and leave a trail of broken hearts behind me.

I was proud of my slender waist, and platinum-blonde hair. My father insisted that I wear a white uniform and waitress shoes to work. How I hated those clumsy shoes! They squeaked like little mice on my skinny ankles. Once, I bought a black uniform with a white ruffled apron, which I thought made me look like an adorable French maid. When I proudly wore my new uniform to work, my father looked at me, gasped, and clasped his hand over his heart like one of the dying Spartans at the battle of Thermopylae.

I stood before the art gallery and visualized my life as a series of selections and reflections. The artwork was intriguing, and the floors were spotless, but the new store seemed empty and impersonal. I studied the display window, focusing on two impressionist paintings. The paintings faded away and instead, for a moment, my father had come to life in my imagination. I envisioned him in the store window. His heavy brows were creased, and his dark eyes were absorbed in his work. As he wiped his hands on his white baker's apron, I visualized his usual attire—a starched white shirt and brown tweed slacks. Moving slowly, but deliberately, he arranged his wares inside the case. One by one, he picked up his confections in his thick hands and assembled them in the shop window.

Stepping back slowly, he studied his work, turned, and added some boxes of fudge and salt-water taffy, creating haphazard, but vivid pyramids. Sometimes I think he was Egyptian. At first the result appeared disorganized, but little by little, he achieved his goal. His image stepped outside and stood beside me. He admired his work and smiled. Then his image vanished. Gone, except in my mind, leaving me to wonder why I was only a bystander to the past.

It all came back to me—my father, the store, and the town where I grew up. I peered into the back of the store where the kitchen used to be. The kitchen was the heart of the business and my father's spirit was doing what he loved best—making candy.

In my mind's eye, I could picture my father slapping a lump of warm taffy on a metal hook, then twisting and pulling until the lump shimmered like a silk gown.

Ghosts of candy makers gathered in the background, laughing as they swirled their wooden paddles through hot caramel until it bubbled like tiny volcanoes. Phantom conversations between my father and his assistant, Teddy Musios, echoed through the walls.

Mr. Musios was a burly, baldheaded man who always sported a wide smile. We addressed him as "Mr. Musios" out of respect. I never saw him angry. To Mr. Musios, it was an honest day's work. He and my father were old friends. I could almost hear their strong voices competing with the whir of the fondant machine. Peanut brittle seethed furiously in its copper kettle, then hissed as it hit the cooling table. I stood aside, listening for the jingle of the tiny bell. I imagined my father's thick hands opening the front door, releasing the smell of cooked peanuts into the air.

This tactic always worked. Little by little, unsuspecting customers drifted into the store.

"What is that wonderful smell?" the customer would ask.

"Oh, that?" I sniffed the air. "That's peanut brittle."

"Peanut brittle? I'll take some of that."

"I've got some cooling right now," I said nonchalantly.

"Can you wait a few minutes? It won't take long."

"Oh, sure. I'm in no hurry."

"Can I get you something else while you're waiting?"

"Oh, yes. I'll take a pound of chocolates; they're just for me."

That was the signal for me to reach under the counter, quickly take out a box, and make a sale. The customer would stand before the case and point to each selection.

"I'll have some of these cashew patties and dark almonds, and oh, these rum creams look good; I like those sprinkles. Oh, and don't forget my favorite—halvah."

"One of my favorites, too!" I'd exclaim. "Of course, everything is my favorite!"

"Don't you get tired of eating candy?"

"No, not *this* candy. This candy is exceptional. It's made with love."

"No wonder it's so good! What is your favorite?"

I'd point to the bottom case.

"Nut mallows."

"See? They're only a cashew patty topped with a big soft marshmallow, then dipped in chocolate. Want to try one?"

"Yes! Thank you!"

I'd hand her the biggest one.

"Delicious," she would exclaim, her mouth unabashedly dribbling chocolate. "I'll take a half pound of those."

She'd smile and I'd do it again. Just like my Uncle George told me: "Always sell them something else."

One thing I liked about the candy store—to make sales. I loved the melodic ring of the gold-filigreed, antique cash register. Whenever I rang up a sale, the round keys sang "ka-ching" and a red arrow popped up on the top. I was happy to ring up the shiny red key, the one labeled "$20." That was a big sale! I would tuck the bills into the little wooden cubby holes where they would wait until my father took them to the bank. In the days before computers, we had to calculate the change in our head. It was easy; we just counted to the given total. The sales would go on all day. Customers would pick out their selections and we would fill their orders.

We knew most of the customers by name and by their favorite candies. Lorraine Newman preferred milk chocolate, Babe Miraglia liked dark-chocolate almonds, and Mrs. Fisch liked cashew patties.

Milk chocolate was the best seller. At Easter we freed chocolate, pink, and white bunnies from their shiny metal molds. The store was packed with Easter baskets, colored eggs, and jellybeans. Customers could order an elaborate chocolate egg for their Easter centerpiece. Each specialty egg was created from two halves of a mold the size of a dinosaur egg. One half was filled with chocolate bunnies, eggs, and Easter grass, then the two halves were sealed together with warm chocolate. The candy makers piped yellow, purple, and pink rosettes on the outside. Tendrils flowed from each rosette, trailing over the chocolate shell like a queen's garden.

I can still see Mrs. Jensen, my father's long-time employee, standing behind the counter, waiting on customers. In those days, we were taught to address adults by their last names. My father always addressed his employee as "Mrs. Jensen," never by "Mildred," her first name. Mrs. Jensen was the epitome of loyalty and patience. She wore her steel-gray hair lightly curled and always held herself with grace and serenity. My restless personality amused Mrs. Jensen. I was a just a scatter-brained kid who couldn't slow down. Even my grandmother called me a flippertyjibbet.

"I don't know what's wrong with me, Mrs. Jensen," I whined. "I wish I could get out of this store and this town forever. All I ever hear about is the candy store. It's impossible to work for family. I never do anything right. I'm sick of waiting on customers. What about me and my life? Nobody really cares about me. That's all I hear day and night: 'the business, the business.' I'm sick of this place and this town. I'm sick of my family. I don't want to spend the rest of my life putting candy in a box!" I'd pout, slamming the empty candy box on the counter. It never occurred to me that Mrs. Jensen spent a good deal of her life putting candy in boxes.

I can still see Mrs. Jensen as she set her work aside and leaned toward me. She smiled, straightened her glasses, and spoke to me calmly: "Now, dear, you don't mean half the things you say. You have a good family, and I'm sure they care about you."

"No, they don't! All they care about is the store. I don't know what's important in life anymore, but it certainly isn't me! How about my life? All they do is focus on the boys, the boys. I wish I had a sister to talk to! Women don't count for much in this family, do they? What am I supposed to do, just get married and have kids?"

"Maybe you will. There's nothing wrong with that. Someday you'll realize what's really important in life. In a very short time, you'll be a woman. You'll have a husband and children of your own. You'll see how hard it is to be a parent. Someday you'll look back and wish you were back here, right behind the counter. You'll see that being a woman carries many, many responsibilities. You can't run away from your responsibilities. Be patient, young lady," she cautioned. "You'll see, you'll see."

"But Mrs. Jensen, I don't want to be just a housewife! I want to be somebody. I want to be important."

"Well, dear, we're all important in our own way."

Mrs. Jensen made a lot of sense, but, of course, I didn't believe a word she said. I never realized how smart Mrs. Jensen was, but her words were prophetic. I finally did discover what's important in life, but I had to lose everything to find it, and I did. I lost everything.

Of my father's many loyal employees, the most interesting were the chocolate dippers. They were masters of a unique profession and a lost art. The dipping room was ice cold, but the ladies didn't mind, especially in summer. They were always talking and laughing as they ran their palms through a puddle of warm chocolate and swirled symbols on their confections.

My mother was a pretty good chocolate dipper, but she warned me, "Never learn to dip chocolates—you'll sit in the dipping room all day." She didn't have to worry. I never could be a chocolate dipper. I just couldn't sit still! I was fifteen, young, and conceited. This was the era of smoldering sensuality, the era of Marilyn Monroe and Elizabeth Taylor. It was the time of Elvis and rock 'n roll. I hoped that someday I would be the next blonde bombshell, but I was skinny and flat-chested.

Mother in front of the store, 1940s

5

My mother's life revolved around creating the perfect family and pleasing that mythical hero—the Greek man. Anastasia, or Yia-Yia, brought my father and his sister Helen to America in 1911 when my father was three years old.

The Sakelaris family were honest, hardworking people. John, my grandfather, worked in a tannery, peddled fruit, and did odd jobs. He quit the tannery when he came home smelling like tannic acid. Later, my grandfather founded his own business, Olympic Bakery. Something tells me the men in the family were either very enterprising or couldn't work for other people. There were nine children in my father's family, eight boys and one girl. Years ago, the industrial town of Lowell, Massachusetts dedicated a park to the seven brothers, who served in WWII.

Angelus, my father, was the eldest child. He was only five foot seven, but he had the presence of an actor. His parents were Greek, but with his olive skin, black wavy hair, and dark eyes, he was often mistaken for Italian or Jewish. These physical attributes heralded acceptance, as my hometown was a melting pot of fascinating and colorful nationalities. The unusual ethnic mix created a vigorous community that contributed to the town's economic and cultural boom.

My father thought he was the new Ulysses, leaving his childhood family at a young age, working in New York, tossed about by the sea of life—fighting everyday monsters, and settling at the Jersey Shore. He saw himself as a smart, self-made man.

It was the summer of 1924, when many of the young Greeks left Lowell to work in New York City for the summer, often working as dishwashers, cooks, and other restaurant jobs. New York City beckoned, but soon the Greeks told my father of a small seaside town called Asbury Park, a bustling community on the Jersey Shore. He spent a summer there and fell in love with it.

My father got a job as a soda jerk on the Asbury Park boardwalk. During this time, he met George Economakis, who we knew as "Uncle George." One day, as my father was scooping out ice cream and George was making fudge, George called my father aside.

"Angy," George asked, "want to learn how to make candy?"

"Well, when can we start?"

"Today."

Soon Uncle George asked my father if he would go partners with him in a candy store. The deal was sealed over a vat of caramel, and so was my fate. In 1933, they opened the original candy store.

Little did they know at the time that a dark cloud was gathering over Germany. My father was oblivious to this spreading terror. While he was busy starting a business, and enjoying his new freedom at the Jersey Shore, Hitler had been proclaimed Chancellor of Germany. Soon a reptilian force, hissing and spewing fire like an unchained dragon, crawled across Europe—shifting the fate not only of Germany, but of humanity.

America was sinking in the Great Depression. Unemployment was high, and bread lines stretched around the corner in many major cities. People were out of a job and out of luck. My father told me that he opened the candy store because he couldn't get a job.

At Christmas, the spicy aroma of cinnamon squares filled the store. Valentine's Day offered a romantic reprieve from the biting cold. The shelves were bursting with pink satin boxes and red velvet hearts.

Uncle George, also known as Mr. Economy, was my godfather. He was the Greek version of Maurice Chevalier, a confirmed bachelor who lived a long, full life. He always dressed impeccably. His white hair, hazel eyes, and blue-gray jacket added a touch of class to the business. He was an innovative businessman who had a talent for waiting on customers and putting people at ease. Every Easter, Uncle George would patiently decorate the Easter baskets with bunnies, jellybeans, and colorful ribbons. No two baskets were alike.

Uncle George told me that the first word he learned in America was sweetheart. In fact, he called all the ladies sweetheart. He even called me sweetheart. George would stand behind the counter, smile and look a blue-haired matron straight in the eye and ask: "What will you have, sweetheart?"

George never said a harsh word about anyone. He told my father, "Angy, you have everything—wife, home, family!"

George welcomed the equality of nationalities. He loved America and seemed to have forgotten his past. He was a unique Greek. George lived in a tiny upstairs apartment accessible by a wrought-iron fire escape. I remember climbing the rickety stairs to his balcony and inhaling the aroma of baked lamb and home-grown roses.

Uncle George was as fascinating and as mysterious as the gold pocket watch that he kept in his jacket. He never left home without his pocket watch. Three or four times a day, he would reach into his pocket, flip open his watch, and note the time. He polished that gold case every day, and whenever he reached for his treasured timepiece, it flashed rays of light.

The watch was beautiful. One day, my feminine curiosity got the best of me.

"Where did you get the watch, Uncle George?"

"Oh, this?" he replied naively, raising his thick white eyebrows that highlighted his matching hair. "I won the watch in a card game—from a Greek sailor."

"I was a young man then, *strong, handsome,*" he said, slapping his chest with his fist.

"I lived way up in the mountains. I traveled down to Athens, then to Piraeus and found a ship going to America. It was a long journey. My father gave me a gold piece for good luck on the journey."

"I used to toss it in the air, like this," he gestured, opening and closing his palm.

"Did you have good luck, Uncle George?"

"Oh, yes. I've been very lucky in life."

"Do you still have the gold piece?"

"Oh, no. I spent it many years ago."

"When did you come to America?"

"Many years ago, on a big, crowded boat. The watch and gold piece were all I had, except for the clothes on my back."

"Did you ever see your father again?"

"No, I never saw my father again. I never went back to Greece."

"Now it's too late," he added.

That was all he would share. He lived in America, in the present.

Uncle George loved the business world and young ladies, even into his old age. He also liked the horses and around 2PM, he would reach inside his suit pocket, lift out the gold watch, flip it open, and check the time. He exited the store quietly, then stood beneath the green awning, shielding himself from the summer sun as he waited for the bus to the racetrack, Monmouth Park. It was midafternoon, but Uncle George always managed to catch the last few horse races. He never married or had children, nor did he own a car or home, but he was a man at peace with both himself and the simple things in life. He lived a good, long life. I admire him to this day.

Funny how you remember people. They just crop up in your subconscious from time to time without any reason. Uncle George and my father had two things in common—being business partners and loving the Jersey Shore.

In the 1950s and 60s, Asbury Park was a jewel by the sea. Sandy beaches, protected by the rocky jetties, stretched the length of the boardwalk. White-lacquered rocking chairs, lulled by ocean breezes, rocked gently on the verandas of stately hotels.

I keep an old photograph of my father, his three brothers, and two cousins as they strolled arm in arm along the Asbury Park boardwalk. The men wore white slacks, and the ladies wore crisp summer dresses. Their smiling faces were so natural that I could almost hear their laughter.

Grand hotels, such as the Berkeley Carteret, stood as sentinels by the sea. At night, couples glided across stately ballrooms, dancing the Peabody, or waltzing to Strauss. Across the street stood Convention Hall, a great stone bastion that jutted out over the ocean.

Like many immigrants, my father was a self-made man. His business came first. Mother was second.

When I was young, Mother liked to wear her favorite gold-filigreed locket around her neck.

"It was my mother's," she assured me.

"Whose picture is in the locket? Dad's?"

"Here—open it," she smiled, handing me the locket.

I snapped the locket open. There was a tiny photo inside, but it wasn't of my father, but of Morgan, our basset hound. His long, floppy ears and big bloodshot eyes looked at me gloomily. Morgan was a sweet, gentle pet, but he sure had a woeful look.

"Mother, it's our dog Morgan! Why do you have a picture of our dog in your locket?"

"He's the only one who loves me."

6

When my parents became engaged, my father took his intended to Lowell to meet *the Greeks*. That's what they were—an elite clan of purebloods. "Fee, fi, fo, fum," they shunned the "blood of an Englishman."

In preparation for this joyous meeting, my mother carefully assembled her wedding trousseau. She was excited about her engagement and anxious to meet my father's family.

Years later, she told me how she packed her favorite pink dress, white blouse, and beige skirt in her old suitcase.

"I dressed conservatively and wanted to make a good impression," she sighed. "I selected my wedding gown at Dainty Apparel, across the street from the candy store."

"Like any woman, I dreamed of being a bride. Your father was much older than I, but I was so proud. I wanted to look my best. All I could do was picture my wedding day. I never had nice clothes unless people gave them to me, or I bought them myself. I put away a little bit of my pay every week to pay for my gown.

"It was an elegant design, a plain white satin gown that fell in soft folds to the floor. I was slimmer then. It fit me beautifully."

Remember the story of the three hundred Spartans who defended the mountainous pass of Thermopylae? Although they weren't Spartans, my father's family was just as formidable. The Greeks were determined to defend my father against the clutches of this fair-haired Nordic intruder. When my mother arrived in Lowell, all the Greeks, except for Papou, voiced their virulent disapproval of my mother. The women swooped down like harpies chattering in an ancient tongue. They resented mother's blonde hair, topaz blue eyes, and stately figure. How dare this crafty goddess seduce their brave Ulysses!

"She isn't Greek!" the family lamented, "How can you do this to us Angy Mou?" the family pleaded, wringing their hands, and weeping into the baklava.

These temperamental Olympians didn't impress my mother. Her family didn't have much, but they were friendly, optimistic people.

She straightened the hem of her pink dress and crossed her ankles politely. Most of the relatives wore black, as if in mourning. Mother tried to smile, wondering what her children would look like. Would they sport thick moustaches? (And that was just the women.)

"Just sit still and be quiet," she chastised herself. Surely the family would come to accept her. Instead, they looked as if they had been eating lemons. The relatives gave her the once over and announced their verdict. It was as if the oracle of Delphi spoke from the depths of the abyss. Supposedly, my mother's fate was sealed.

Don't get me wrong. My father's relatives were good, hardworking people. That's just the way things were back then, hypocritical. People focused on economics and ethnicity. Some people are like that today. Besides, a young woman and an older man is often the object of speculation.

Only one person gave my father his blessing—his father, John. Papou was the patriarch of the family and the only family member to approve the match.

Papou took my father aside and whispered, "She's beautiful! Marry her!"

There was an uneasy stillness on the drive home to New Jersey. My father's resolution crumbled to his knees like the columns of the Parthenon. Nearing Gran's home, he grew quiet.

The next day he called my mother, and sadly announced: "I can't marry you."

"Why?" my mother exclaimed, panicking.

"You're not Greek."

"Not Greek! Angy, of course I'm not Greek! You knew that. I can't be something I'm not!"

"It's your family, isn't it?"

"Yes."

My mother wasn't Greek? Well, what a surprise! How could my father have mistaken my mother's family for Greeks? I guess my father wasn't too observant the first time he visited my mother's house for dinner. When Gran served him loin of pork and sauerkraut, didn't my father realize he was a long way from the taverna?

My mother's shoulders sagged, and she began to weep. My father called off the wedding. Mother sank into depression. Her plans of marriage and a new life became the dark ending in a fairytale. She didn't even have the heart to return her wedding gown, so it sat forgotten, tucked away in her tiny bedroom closet like a crumpled tissue.

When Gran met my father's family, she was convinced they were a throwback to Neanderthals. Even so, it was Gran who phoned my father a few months after Angy broke the engagement. My mother had collapsed and was admitted to the hospital. She had been sobbing incoherently.

Angy gave in. He humbled himself and visited the hospital with a dozen red roses. Humility doesn't happen much in a Greek family. My father disregarded his relatives' advice and asked Mother to marry him. Fifty years later, when my father was ill, Mother sent a dozen red roses to the hospital. My father wept unashamedly.

My mother always displayed the old black and white portrait of her wedding day in the living room. I still have the portrait; it's the only item I wanted from my mother's home. In the photo, Mother is draped in a demure, ivory satin gown. A lush bouquet of antique roses graced her hands.

The Second World War had broken out, and though my father was in his thirties, he was drafted. My mother protested, but to no avail. When chocolate and sugar were rationed during the war, Mother bought Hershey bars to melt for chocolate and hand-dipped the chocolates herself.

My father was still serving in the South Pacific in 1944 when I was born. Soon the blissful honeymoon began to sour. The difficulties of maintaining a home and business in wartime began to take their toll.

My father returns home, 1945

My mother felt abandoned once again. She had been in labor for two days, and I was born with the umbilical cord wrapped around my neck. The doctor cleared his throat and announced that he had just delivered a similar birth, but the baby died.

I often ask myself why God chose to let me live. God must have chosen me to do something important in life. You know the saying, "Next time, God, choose someone else."

Gran told me that, after I was born, my mother was sick for a "few months." It may have been postpartum depression. Years later, Mother told me she was just exhausted from the demands of keeping house, the new baby, and working in the store.

In those days, if a woman went to a doctor, the doctor assumed the woman was a hypochondriac or malingerer. If the woman was pretty, the doctor assumed that the woman was "looking for attention." I wonder how many physicians suffered from similar medical narrow mindedness.

I was truly my mother's daughter. I keep an old baby photo of my mother and me in my photo album. We were smiling and looking into the camera. My mother's golden hair was styled in a pompadour, while wisps of blonde hair stuck up on my forehead, forming a soft curl. It's one of the few pictures of us together.

By 1943, Germany was struggling to win the war. Germany had planned to establish Germania, a new world order that would last a thousand years. I was just a year old on the morning of September 2, 1945, the day the Japanese surrendered to the Allies. Recently, I saw an old photo of the surrender. As the battleship *Missouri* sat silently at anchor in Tokyo Bay, representatives of the Japanese government boarded the ship. Since the Japanese had accepted the Allied terms of surrender weeks before, the ceremony was merely a formality. Some Japanese officers wore white gloves and military uniforms, others wore dark suits, starched white shirts, and tall black hats. Their dark clothes and stoic expressions reflected the solemnity of the moment.

Over thirty military brass and personnel stood in a semicircle behind them. The Americans looked as solemn as the Japanese. The Americans were dressed in khaki uniforms and the American generals seemed almost casual. The Japanese stood by like ghosts. No one was smiling.

The war having ended, my father returned home. He spoke sadly of his visit to Hiroshima and the horrific scene of destruction.

The war's end, in August of 1945, brought a wave of rebirth and prosperity to our country. The servicemen and women returned home and started families. Women gained respectability both in the military and the home front. However, my mother resented the fact that her husband had been away when she had needed him the most.

And what did he ask? "Where's all the money?"

Mother and baby Joanie, 1945

7

One characteristic of Greek tragedy is how the hero stubbornly follows his own overwhelming pride, or *hubris,* on his proud path to destruction while the audience looks on in anguish.

Besides being a talented candy maker, my father was a great storyteller.

"What story would you like to hear tonight?" he would ask.

Even though I was only nine years old, the answer was always the same: "Tell me the story of Ulysses."

The *Odyssey* was my favorite story. Night after night, warriors, goddesses, and sea monsters came to life. It was an awesome cast of characters for such a young mind. Naturally the Greeks always won, and their cleverness was impressive.

My father's voice grew solemn.

"After the Trojans dragged the wooden horse inside the city gates, they started celebrating. Soon, they were drinking and carousing until they fell asleep. The Greek soldiers, who had been hiding in the wooden horse, climbed down the ladder and attacked the Trojans, killing them or driving them into the sea.

"Do you know what happened next?"

"Yes, the Greeks burned Troy to the ground."

"Good! I see you remember."

I was fascinated by Helen of Troy.

"What did Helen of Troy look like?" I asked.

"Look like? Well, she was blonde, blue-eyed, and beautiful. She held her head high, like this," he gestured, "like an aristocrat."

"Like my mother?"

"Well, yes, like your mother."

My father's voice rose dramatically. He waved his hand dramatically into the air, and his eyes took on a faraway stare, as if looking into another dimension. He paused, then continued.

"Helen of Troy had the 'face that launched a thousand ships.'"

I couldn't imagine how one woman could possess such charm, beauty, and power. I pictured my mother as Helen of Troy, the lovely young queen married to an older Menelaus. Years later, my husband told me that I "had a face that launched a thousand diners."

The ancient Greeks seemed to have great insight into the heart and psyche of the human mind. They recognized and feared the strength and power of women.

Gods and goddesses populated my dreams. I had nightmares of Medusa, a once beautiful woman now changed into a hideous snake-headed Gorgon whose glance turned men into stone.

How I admired Penelope, Ulysses' faithful wife. I envisioned myself draped in a flowing white peplos, my long hair polished with scented oil and sculpted into a simple chignon. I could almost feel the cool marble tiles beneath my bare feet. I may not have been beautiful, but I knew I could fill the role of the long-suffering, dutiful wife. All day I would weave my tapestry and greet my suitors, but every night I would unravel my work, one thread at time.

Night after night, the myths unfolded. While other children listened to Bible stories, I absorbed Greek drama. Even as a child, I realized that the *Odyssey* was a myth that had been passed down to each generation. I realized that I was the next generation to hear the stories.

Naturally, I realized that there were no real gods and goddesses, but the story had subtle insights into human nature. Fate, I learned, was a vital theme in Greek drama.

Oedipus Rex was one of my father's favorite plays. This was no fairytale. After Oedipus became the king of Thebes, a curse fell on the town, and Oedipus searched for the answer to the curse. In his arrogance, he discovered the truth. Oedipus himself had unwittingly murdered his father and married his own mother.

My father couldn't resist dramatizing the scene when Oedipus had his apotheosis.

"Do you know what Oedipus did next?"

My eyes widened. I searched the room for an answer. None came. I didn't know what to expect.

My father's eyes widened. Slowly he raised his hands. I watched in horror as he held them high, like talons, and turned them inward toward his face. Swiftly he brought them toward his eyes, as if he were an eagle, swooping down on its hapless prey.

I grew silent as he knit his heavy brows together.

"When Oedipus discovered the truth, he went mad. He grabbed his mother's brooch and gouged his eyes out—like this!"

He thrust his palms over his eyelids and ran his fingers down his face.

"And then," he hesitated, "Oedipus went blind."

I shuddered at the thought.

This was too much for a child to comprehend.

"You see," my father continued, "Oedipus and his family were cursed forever."

He spoke softly as he quoted the end of the play:

> Citizens of our ancestral Thebes, look on this Oedipus, the mighty and once masterful, elucidator of the riddle, envied on his pedestal of fame.
>
> You saw him fall; you saw him swept away. So, being mortal, look on that last day and count no man blessed in his life until he's crossed life's bounds unstruck by ruin still.

8

In reality, much of my life reminded me of a cross between a Greek tragedy and a Tennessee Williams play. I looked at myself in the mirror. I had blonde hair and a nice figure. I was popular, or at least I thought I was. I even pretended to be dumb. My father told me that men didn't like women who were smarter than them. I was beginning to like attention from boys, and my mother encouraged me to develop my femininity. Why? To find a rich husband. This was my mother's goal for me, to marry a rich man. This was confusing because my father wanted me to be a waitress. My father's dream was for me to marry a Greek boy, have nine children, and live over a restaurant.

Allenhurst was Interlaken's neighboring town. Great tiled-roof mansions rose up along the ocean, forming an enclave reminiscent of *The Great Gatsby*. The community was mostly Scotch and Irish, with names like Sullivan, O'Keefe, and McCaffery.

Mostly, I remember Dennis and Barry, the Considine boys. They had their own band, and they were happy to play for free at my sixteenth birthday party. We had the party at my house, but we never told my father, as he would not have allowed it.

I'll never forget my father's face when he drove up unexpectedly, saw the cars, and heard the music. My mother

calmed him down and introduced him to the band. He liked their music, and he was surprised to learn that they were the sons of Bob Considine, the famous columnist. My father told them that they could play until 9 PM, and at nine on the dot, they packed up their instruments and left. He always told the story of how the Considine boys kept their word.

Mother would "ooh" and "aah" whenever a prospective suitor graced our front steps. One of her favorite suitors was John Sauer, a popular Allenhurst teen who drove a beige coupe, wore a straw hat, and knew all the words to the Kingston Trio songs. John was a fun-loving student known for his high school pranks. He had gained notoriety by tackling a local police officer who was chasing him for disorderly conduct. John merely did an about-face and tackled the officer.

John's father was a prominent dentist. Visions of beach clubs, country clubs, and cocktail parties flashed before my mother's eyes. None of that impressed me.

I can still picture John as he walked up to my front door. He had a slight swagger but stopped to steady his straw hat and pull up his madras shorts.

"Here comes John!" my mother exclaimed, while she channeled up spirits of *The Glass Menagerie* and the promise of a gentleman caller.

I never knew whether John came over to take me out or have a drink, but I have a good idea.

"Here, John, have a drink," Mother proposed, flinging open the doors to the liquor cabinet.

"Mother!" I exclaimed, as John grinned wildly. John was only seventeen-and-a-half years old. I was embarrassed, but this was understandable. My family was always trying to pawn me off in the name of prosperity. I was mortified.

John was the quintessential preppie, but I never did find out whether he went to college. Last I heard, he and his brother owned a successful bar in San Francisco. The last time I saw John was at my husband's class reunion. He was wearing a huge tie that fell all the way to the floor. He felt no pain. I never understood what he saw in me, but I have a good idea. Whenever I hear the Kingston Trio singing, "Sloop John B," or "Scotch and Soda," I think of John, the preppie.

Since my parents wanted me to marry a rich man, I did what every teenager before me has done. I defied them. I began a romance with one of the poorest young men I could find.

His name was Mike, and he was my first real boyfriend. I met him in the fall of 1959, when I was a sophomore in Asbury Park High School, and he was returning for graduate studies. Mike was an all-round tough guy. He stood 5'11, had black, shiny hair, played football, and was built like a Greek god (or maybe a Greek devil). Obviously, Mike wasn't Greek. He was Italian. I knew this would get a rise out of my parents. My rebellion would be complete.

I first noticed Mike in the school library when he was sitting in the back of the library with his friends, the King boys. My friends and I were studying quietly, when all of a sudden, someone set off a round of firecrackers.

"Pop! Pop! Pop!" We thought the Russians had launched an attack on Asbury Park High School. Everyone except Mike and the King boys jumped in their chairs. Miss Schnell, the ultimate librarian, was calm as a schoolmarm. She didn't break a sweat.

"Everyone gather your books and line up, please. The bell will ring in five minutes."

My friends and I got in line. I was the third person away from Mike. I couldn't help but notice him. He was leaning against the wall, under a picture of George Washington. Since Washington was the father of our country, this seemed to be a good omen. I thought to myself, "Could this be the father of my children?" We could create our own dynasty of confused nationalities. I felt a warm feeling spreading across my flat chest. It fanned out to my neck and arms until my face flushed like a Jersey tomato. Maybe it was measles. What a pubescent twit I was, a real dumb bunny.

It was September, and Mike's short sleeves displayed his well-toned muscular arms and slim waist. His white shirt was neatly tucked into his black pegged pants, and his white socks peeked out from the top of his black shoes. Mike's bronze, ruddy complexion, and a spiky, flattop haircut contrasted his white shirt. His green eyes brooded with Celtic melancholy, while his dark skin and powerful build heralded ancient Rome. The dopey fifteen-year-old girl in me stumbled and fell, as the blonde goddess raced ahead, scooping up the golden apple and leaving childhood behind. Puberty had made me delusional.

Mike shifted his weight from one foot to another. He never even noticed me. Visions of Heathcliff, Rhett Butler, and Ulysses flashed before my eyes. I felt an emptiness in my stomach. He was ignoring me. My opportunity to be the faithful, long-suffering Penelope may have been lost forever. My future martyrdom almost eluded me.

I pictured myself standing before the iconostasis of the Greek Church. My white lace gown trailed over the altar as the choir sang Byzantine hymns. The priest ceremoniously raised two pearled crowns over our heads. My breath came in short gasps. I met Mike's gaze, but he looked away. The crowns fell. The choir faded.

Then the bell rang.

This daydream would have been forgotten if it hadn't been for the following afternoon in study hall. I never thought I would see Mike again. In fact, I didn't even know his name. By accident I was sitting in the auditorium with my best friend, Nancy. This was supposed to be study hall, but very few students studied in study hall, a tradition that has been carefully preserved. Mike was sitting with the King boys. Suddenly, Nancy and I turned to see Mike stand up, grab a folding chair, and hit Bobby King over the head with it. This produced a sense of chaos, and for a moment we thought a fight would break out. Just as two male teachers rushed to the front of the auditorium, the bell rang.

The bells kept ringing: could they be wedding bells?

Uh-oh. Mike had caught my eye again.

No matter how old we become, we will always remember our loved ones as we first met them. No matter how sick, how

debilitated they become, we insist on envisioning them as strong and vigorous. That sick, disabled person inhabiting our loved one's body must be an imposter. Although the outward appearance has changed, the same spirit you once loved inhabits their body.

Mike must have noticed me. How could I have missed that sly, lizard-eyed once over? What did I know about men? I was a sophomore—Mike was a senior. I went on, stumbling to meet my fate.

It's the façade that attracts us, or maybe the lack of it. What conceit drives us to chase this façade of another human being, that essence we seek to capture and claim as ours alone? The force draws us, buoyed by the salt sea, until we are swept away, where we either catch the waves to shore, or flounder and drown. Our egotism drives us to possess another's strength and weakness and mold it into our being, our oneness, and our soul. Do we really love this illusion the other represents, or do we selfishly seek to desire that which is needed to complete our own being?

Only when our loved one is truly stripped of that illusion, can we see the spirit within—the true essence that God has revealed to us. Surprisingly, we can love someone more deeply in illness than in health. We are overwhelmed as our loved one grasps for survival, helplessly seeking our intercession. We step back, awed by that which we have no control over, and enlightened by the fact that our loved one always kept a corner of his or her life hidden from us—obscured by ego. We realize that we, too, have a part of us hidden from the world. In our weakness we glimpse some deep truth, not only of the suffering of others, but also of our own, and all humanity.

Thank goodness for friends. Friends are always there to guide you, advise you, and ruin your life. I really believe my friend Nancy either had ESP or a remarkable ability to predict success.

Nancy had a crush on Mike's friend, Richie.

"Richie's kind of' cute, don't you think?" she whispered.

"Who's he?"

"His name is Richie. He's one of the King boys. His brother Roger is good-looking too."

"Who are the King boys?" I asked.

"Oh, they're just some boys who are gonna' be somebody someday."

"What do you mean?"

"You'll see, you'll see," she smiled, tossing her long blonde hair.

One thing about Nancy, people listened when she spoke. I always thought Nancy was one of my smartest friends, not only because she'd say things and they would happen. Nancy lived in a cozy Tudor home in West Allenhurst. Her father, Edward, was a prominent stockbroker with the New York Stock Exchange. Edward was a quiet, straightforward, and conservative man. He was a widower, and Nancy was only eight when she lost her mother. Edward hired a young woman named Margaret to oversee the household, and Margaret became a lifetime motherly figure to Nancy and her sister, Deanne.

Nancy epitomized success and class. When Nancy said that Richie's friend Mike wanted to go out with me, I listened.

"Me? Somebody wants to go out with me?"

This amazed me because a boy had just broken up with me. I didn't miss going parking in the boondocks on Saturday nights and watching my ex-boyfriend drink beer, but my ego was crushed. Now this rugged hunk of manhood wanted to go out with me.

"What did this guy say about me?"

"Mike asked Richie to ask me who my knock-kneed, pigeon-toed little friend was," Nancy confided.

What a compliment.

"I won't go out with him," I frowned.

"Why not?"

"I don't know. He looks a lot older than me."

"Don't be silly. Who else asked you out?"

"Nobody."

"Then you'll go out with him?"

"Well, maybe."

"Then it's settled."

I made a face.

"OK, if you say so."

Nancy was more sophisticated than I was, so I blindly followed her suggestion. I went out with Mike. It was Friday night and Mike's friend Frankie drove us to the movies to see *Mogombo*. Afterward we walked to Freddie's Pizzeria to have pizza. My stomach was jumping so much I could hardly eat. Mike was strong, proud, and street-smart, and I was an insecure adolescent.

I knew I could never fill my mother's size-nine heels, so I thought it would be a great stroke of independence if I brought this dark hero into the provincialism of my mother's home.

So began my odyssey into womanhood.

It all depends on how you look at it—my dark mythic hero, or villain, was about to enter the story. Mike was ruggedly handsome. Too many novels and too many myths were spinning in my head. I envisioned my parent's reaction as I dragged this flawed hero home. It was the old tale of beauty taming the beast. I could hardly wait to open the door and watch my parent's reaction to this embodiment of masculinity. Would they be impressed? I could see their eyes widen in amazement. Their shy, skinny huntress had brought home a stag.

It was the fall of 1959. The first blush of autumn brought Indian summer to the Jersey Shore. Soon the warm weather would cool the vibrant yellow and crimson oaks and the sweet fragrance of burning leaves would fill the night air, hurtling sparks into the air like fireflies. Pep rallies popped up overnight as crackling red bonfires illuminated the night sky, scattering wisps of blue and gold into the darkness.

It was October, but Indian summer brought warm sun and soft summer winds to the Jersey Shore. One afternoon, Mike asked me to walk down to the beach with him after school. It was only three short blocks from the school. I noticed that Mike didn't smile much; he seemed very serious for such a young man. I wondered what he thought about, or whether he liked me or not. He always seemed deep in thought, almost edgy, as if someone were stalking him, ready to jump out of the shadows and ambush him. Nervously, he turned his eyes away from me as he scanned the street for trouble.

Mike was unique, but a woman's voice inside me said: "Yes, he has potential." I wanted to shine him up like a new penny. There was some autonomy in his rebel stance that attracted me. The ocean's glare blinded us as we scanned the empty horizon. Waves splashed on shore and trickled between the craggy rocks, dragging tendrils of deep green moss into the sea. It was a quiet, innocent afternoon.

Mike spread a blanket across the soft sand.

"Where do you live, Mike?"

"Asbury Avenue," he said, almost frowning. "Across from Mount Carmel Church."

Mount Carmel was a great stone church that loomed over the nondescript neighborhood across the tracks. The church was a bastion of Italian Catholicism. I was surprised that Mike had been an altar boy and attended mass regularly.

"I like your hair," he said suddenly, changing the subject.

"You do?"

No one ever said they liked my hair.

"Yeh, it's nice—blonde.

"You're like a princess—a little princess."

I dug my feet deeper in the sand to keep from falling over. Suddenly the sea was pounding in my head. The gulls shrieked and cried like white ravens while I was swimming in his green eyes.

Princess? No one ever called me a princess.

I thought I was a boxer. I boxed chocolates. My father was more concerned with whether I boxed his chocolates correctly.

"Remember," he would insist, "when you box chocolates, it's dark, light, dark, light and four across. Seven rows down. That makes twenty-eight."

"Can you remember that?"

Meanwhile, my mother wanted me to stay home and help her wax the china cabinet. My brothers stole my diary, put a frog under my pillow, and asked me to don shoulder pads and play football with them.

Mike and I were inseparable. It was the ultimate rebellion, the girl from the "perfect home" meets the tough guy from Asbury Avenue.

I envisioned myself rising, like Botticelli's Venus, from the sea of childhood.

My childhood friends faded away. The carefree days of climbing trees, playing hopscotch and tag vanished forever. The country was celebrating its adolescence. Rock 'n roll, the frenzied revolution of the young, was the craze. On Saturday nights, students gathered at the high school gym for dances, or "canteens." Songs such as "Earth Angel" and "Sixteen Candles" echoed through the halls. Girls wore crinolines and flats, saddle shoes, and full skirts. We tied scarves around our ponytails or styled our hair in a French roll. We snuggled innocently to a slow dance, our flats barely scuffing the floor. The chaperones would roll their eyes as our poodle skirts twirled to the fast beat of a jitterbug. We danced, talked, and flirted like young coquettes.

By now I was wearing Mike's ring on a chain around my neck, which meant we were going steady. The style at the time included cashmere sweaters, pleated skirts, and stockings fastened with floppy garter belts that pinched small round indentations in our young thighs. Preppies wore chinos and madras. The Marlon Brando look was still popular. Teens wore leather jackets and scrunched cigarette packs under the sleeves of their T-shirts. The pungent smell of perfume and pomade mingled with the resin of freshly lacquered floors.

I can still feel the cool air and visualize the chaperones standing guard by the gymnasium door. I can still hear the scratchy record grinding out the lyrics: "Just two kinds of people in the world... a boy and girl."

Would be tough guys asked perky schoolgirls to dance. We gazed into our partner's eyes in innocence, glorying in our adolescence. Like most teens, we had a naïve view of love. We lived on pizza, burgers, and soda. Nobody worried about cholesterol or drank bottled water. Freddie's Pizzeria was the big hangout after the dances—a place where we could meet friends, flirt, and munch on pizza until our arteries swelled with mozzarella cheese.

We women never leave well enough alone, do we? I decided that Mike was a diamond in the rough who needed a little polishing. I thought I could do the polishing.

I thought I could change him, so I invited him home to meet my family.

Mike pulled up to the front door in his gray 1948 Cadillac. The rumor was that Mike had won a Cadillac in a card game down on Springwood Avenue. Somehow, I pictured a white 1959 Cadillac with whitewalls and red upholstery. Well, it was a Cadillac all right, but instead of a plush Caddy, Mike pulled up in a clunker. It was primed a dull, drab gray and was as wide as a river barge. One hubcap was missing, and the windows were as dark and as narrow as a mud hut. The muffler rattled and smoke puffed out of the tailpipe. It was the ugliest car I had ever seen.

When my mother peeked out the window, I could see her eyes widen in horror. "Look at his car! What will the neighbors think?"

Mike strode up to the front door with confidence and rang the bell.

Mother peeked out the window again.

"You *can't* go out with him!" she hissed.

"*What? Why not*?" I hissed back. "I've been going out with him for four whole months."

"He's too old for you! Much too old!"

"Too old? He's only *three* years older than me. My father is thirteen years older than you!"

"Yes, but he's your father."

"Mother! You're married to a man thirteen years older than you!"

"Yes, but your boyfriend is Italian—a foreigner! The other boys won't ask you out. He's practically an immigrant!"

"Mother, Mike was born in America, and so was I. Besides, did you forget that *my* father was born in Greece? Greece and Italy are neighbors! They're right across from each other on the Mediterranean."

"Neighbors? Well, I never thought of that."

Mother peeked through the curtains again.

"Well, he *is* well dressed. Nice suit. Good-looking, too."

Mike straightened his sharkskin jacket and stood firmly in his featherweight shoes. He did look a lot older than me, but then again, Mother liked older men, so maybe it was a family tradition.

Mother smoothed her skirt, turned, and quietly opened the door. This was a good sign because my father once slammed the door on a prospective suitor.

Mike walked in with all the confidence of a Sumo wrestler.

"Hello, Mrs. Sakelaris," he said politely, while ceremoniously handing her a bouquet of gold mums.

"Mom, this is Mike. Mike, this is Mom," I said proudly. My mother's face said it all. She was losing her daughter.

"Nice to meet you," Mike nodded with all the refinement he could muster.

I could imagine what he was thinking: "Gee, this girl's mother is beautiful!"

My mother fixed him with her blue eyes.

"Where do you live?"

"Asbury Park."

"Oh, yes, we have a candy store there."

"I know. The Caramel Shop has the best candy in town."

Mike was a lot smarter than I thought.

It was the beginning of a new relationship.

Suddenly I saw my mother in a new light. Suddenly she became a threat to my independence and womanhood. Was it my mother who changed or was it me? Soon I would drift away from the family, and Mother would turn her attention toward my younger brothers.

My father was unperturbed by my new love. His immediate reaction was, "Can't you find a Greek boy?"

"Why do I have to 'find a Greek boy,' Dad?" I whined.

"Because you are *Greek*! I am your father, and I am Greek. You live in my house and eat my food. You are Greek. I will find you a Greek boy."

I sighed. I began to realize that if Quasimodo came to the door and told us he was Greek, my father would welcome him as my betrothed, wedding bells and all.

After a while, my father tolerated my new infatuation and stopped walking out of the room when Mike arrived.

"At least he has a job," was my father's only compliment. "He can support you someday," he sighed. That was his main goal in life, finding someone to support me, as he maintained that I was a great burden on the family. What was I to do? Dad had regaled me with tales of Ulysses until I sought out my own mythic wanderer. I felt a power well up inside me, the power of a young woman to mold and transform both my flawed hero and myself.

9

It was the fall of 1959. It may have been the fall of Mike and me. We embarked on the road to downward mobility. Although Mike and I came from different backgrounds, we both grew up in the small town of Asbury Park, attended high school there, loved rock 'n roll and the Jersey Shore. Mike's father was Italian; mine was Greek. Mike's mother was a faded Irish beauty; mine was a Nordic beauty. Our fathers both came from large, close, Mediterranean families who considered their wives outsiders. Each family had only one daughter. My father and grandfather had been in the bakery business, Mike's family delivered bread. Our mothers' vanishing charms were leading them down Sunset Boulevard. Finally, in a twist of fate, years later, our mothers would suffer nervous breakdowns within months of each other.

Mike grew up on Asbury Avenue, in a friendly Italian neighborhood where everyone knew each other. He lived catty-cornered to Mount Carmel Church, a red brick edifice that stood guard over the small community. Would-be tough guys straight out of *Rebel Without a Cause* hung out at Bocky's corner store. Future movie stars such as Danny De Vito and Vic Morrow lived down the street. Weekend gathering places for teens, such as Freddie's Pizzeria and Horner's Drive-In, were nearby. Mike and his friend Frankie played sports at the Boy's Club, two blocks away.

The neighborhood was full of interesting characters. Most of them had nicknames. Mike's friend, "Jimmy Nik-Nik," had some type of speech impediment that made him stutter and earned him his nickname, but the other kids accepted him as one of the gang. Jimmy was strong for his age, but he had this fantasy that he was really Superman in disguise. One day the gang challenged him to prove his claim.

They pointed to one of the cars by the curb and challenged him: "Jimmy, if you're really Superman, let's see you lift this car."

Jimmy Nik-Nik grabbed the fender and tried to lift the car. He huffed and puffed, but he couldn't budge the car.

"What happened Jimmy?" they asked knowingly.

Jimmy wiped his hands on his shirt.

"I d-don't know. The car must have k-k-ryptonite in it."

Mike's house stood in the middle of the block. The homes were varied in style, some featured porches and wooden steps. Most homes were built in the 1920s and 1930s. The yards were small. Mike had an old chicken coop in the back yard and a dilapidated garage filled with the previous tenant's keepsakes. The house was connected to the back of a storefront that didn't sell much except a few loaves of Italian bread, soda, and odds and ends at inflated prices. Once a week, men met in the backroom to play cards and shoot dice. On Friday nights, their shouts could be heard through the thin walls of Mike's rented house.

I was very apprehensive about meeting Mike's parents. For a moment, I hesitated as I took a step toward the house. The cement sidewalk was overgrown with thick weeds, but there, in the center of the lawn, rising from the depths, was a glorious rose bush. The leaves were a glossy green, and the red roses blushed in the warmth of Indian summer. The stems, thick with thorns, had momentarily triumphed over the weeds. The bush was too magnificent to touch.

"It's my mother's favorite rosebush," Mike announced, his eyes looking down on the gravel. A cool breeze rustled the thorny branches. The soft petals wept onto the ground. I wanted to pick a rose, but I left it alone, lest the petals fall apart in my hands.

As I looked up at the crumbling steps and peeling paint, I felt a sense of defeat. The rose bush was a beauty in a world of weeds.

As he led me up to the front door, I had an overpowering sense of sickness and wasted lives. Mike led me down a dusty hallway cluttered with wastebaskets and garden tools. We emerged into a small living room complete with a sagging brown sofa, one beige chair, and two spindly end tables that looked as if they needed a walker to lean on. Beside the rickety banister stood a small television, its rabbit ears protruding into the stillness. A doorway on the left opened to a large, comfortable kitchen. A new refrigerator stood out against the wall, while a big, round table hugged the corner. A large gas range stood against the wall, its black burners silent and cold.

Mike's parents' bedroom was down the hallway from the kitchen. The room was clean and neat, with an air of melancholy about it. In the corner stood a distressed maple dresser. There was only one picture in the room, a faded black and white photo of a young woman in a gray lace-collared dress. Within the frame, the young woman smiled sweetly at me. Her dark upswept hair framed her oval face, and her delicate hands were clasped coquettishly beneath her chin. I picked up the picture and held it toward the light.

"That's my mother," Mike said softly. "She was very beautiful," he continued, "until she got sick."

"She's lovely," I said with a smile.

"My mother had long black hair and green eyes. Hair to her waist. She's Irish. Her name was Nolan."

"She's an Irish beauty."

"Well, she was. . ." Mike trailed off.

"Hey, want a sandwich? Do you like baloney and cheese? We always have cheese—sometimes ham if we're lucky. Let's go to the kitchen, I'll fix it for you."

Mike led me back to the kitchen.

"Sit down," he gestured, as he opened the door to the refrigerator.

"My sister just bought this new refrigerator."

He opened the refrigerator, grabbed two slices of yellow cheese and two pieces of baloney, and slapped them between two pieces of bread. Then he slipped it on a paper plate and handed it to me as if it were a gourmet meal.

"This is just commercial bread. My father sells the best bread—Italian bread. Baldanza Bread, it's fresh, too. My father delivers it. We always have fresh bread."

"Want some mayonnaise? Mustard?"

"Yes, please."

"Got it right here, bottom shelf."

"Thanks, I'll have mayonnaise," I nodded, peeking into the refrigerator.

There wasn't much food, just a battered pot of spaghetti sauce, a hunk of provolone cheese, and some fresh eggs on the second shelf. The bottom shelf held heads of lettuce, garlic, olives, and three green peppers. A bottle of milk stood alone on the top shelf.

"Oh, that's buttermilk. Want some? My mother loves it," Mike explained, noting my curiosity.

We ate our sandwiches in silence.

Somehow the baloney-and-cheese sandwich tasted pretty good. I guess I was hungry.

"Want to see my room? It's upstairs, next to my sister's room. I'll show you."

We walked together up the creaky stairs. I noticed that one of the rails in the banister was missing. The room was tiny and cold, but there was a bed, table, and dresser. I pushed the faded curtain aside. The small window looked out over a rundown garage, a rabbit hutch, and an enormous vegetable garden.

Mike cleared his throat. "My room's small; my sister has the nice room. She's neat, I'm messy," he said, laughing nervously.

"Oh," I sighed, thinking of the tranquility of my own room, my white and gold matching dressing table and carved mirror. I thought of my view, my white curtains rising and falling in the breeze as I watched the morning sun as it sparkled on the nearby lake. I let the curtain fall.

"Well, this is it," he concluded. "Let's go downstairs."

We walked back down the creaky stairs and sat on the lumpy sofa. Then Mike walked over to an old desk, yanked on a crooked drawer, and clutched a dog-eared album.

"See this picture?" he asked, opening the album.

"This is my mom; she's holding me in her arms."

He pointed to a faded black and white photo.

"See what the caption says? 'First baby born on December 7, 1941'."

I looked closely and felt uneasy. A lovely, smiling young woman was bent over a newborn baby. Her long, dark hair was swept about her head as she proudly cradled the baby in her delicate arms. Her thick eyelashes brushed her fair cheeks, lending a Madonna and child quality to the photo.

"Here's another picture of my mother and me. See? She had such beautiful, black hair."

"Once we owned a house, a nice house. It was around the corner," he added.

"What happened?"

"My father lost it in a card game."

"What? That isn't even legal!"

"They said we could stay, but they kicked us out. It happened a long time ago. Now we rent this house."

My concept of gamblers was limited to old movies and Broadway musicals. I had visions of Nathan Detroit in *Guys and Dolls*.

"My father is a gambler. He's always trying to win enough money to buy us a house."

We heard the creaking of the kitchen door.

A voice called softly from the kitchen door: "Mike, are you home? Mike? Could you come here?"

"I'll be right there, Mom. Hold on."

He hopped toward the kitchen and grabbed a small bag of groceries from his mother's frail hands.

"I got it Mom. I got it!" He said, grabbing the bag just before it fell to the ground.

"Whew! I'm tired!" she breathed, flopping down on a kitchen chair.

"I walked all the way from the corner. . ."

"Mom, you know you have trouble walking since you fell. Why didn't you tell me you were going to the store?"

"I wanted to do it myself."

She placed her wrists palms down on the table, but quickly turned them over. Her wrists were slender and graceful, yet her nails were bitten down to the quick. I looked into her soft green eyes. They were as faded as a stray cat. Dyed-black hair, peppered with gray, hung in wisps about her pale skin. Even so, hardship and sickness couldn't dim her beautiful skin. Her face was so opalescent that it gave the impression that pearls were snuggling under her skin.

"Yes, Mom, I'm here. There's someone I want you to meet."

I got up from sofa and walked to the kitchen table. My empty plate sat unceremoniously in front of me.

"Mom, this is Joanie."

"Joanie, this is my mother, Ruth."

I took a step forward.

"Glad to meet you, Mrs. Corcione," I smiled.

"Call me Ruth, everybody calls me Ruth."

"Well, nice to meet you, Ruth. That's a pretty name."

A look of surprise flickered across my face, but my fading tan concealed the slight flush spreading across my cheeks. Ruth was a silhouette of the woman she had been.

Mike's mother gave a half smile, as if she knew what I was thinking.

I must have looked puzzled. There wasn't a wrinkle on her face.

"Ruth, your skin is beautiful!"

She cleared her throat and spoke in a modest voice.

"Thank you. I always use cold cream at night. It's natural."

She looked away, then studied her hands. They were trembling slightly.

"I think I'll go rest," she said quietly, holding onto the table for support.

"I'll help you, Mom."

"No, I'm fine." She pushed her frail arms against the table and walked unsteadily to her room.

"I hope you're OK, Mom."

"Yeah, I'm fine. Have a little trouble walking, that's all."

"What's wrong?" I whispered.

"We don't know. She has trouble walking. Her mother had the same problem, but it didn't show up until later in life. Hope I don't get it."

The woman before me swayed like a stranger emerging from a fog. The stranger's eyes were sunken into dark circles, her skin was framed with dusky, brittle curls, and her lips were dry and cracked. An air of resignation clung to her like vinegar. A phantom had besieged a bright and gentle spirit.

There was something more familiar to me. Her faded green eyes spoke of illness, both physical and emotional. A wild Irish rose fading away. Mike's mother was concealing pain, pain that stiffened her hands and arms and weakened her legs. Her hands shook visibly, but her face told the story. Pain was ravaging her, crippling her from within. She had accepted her fate, like an ancient Irish curse. Still, I could see where Mike got his good looks from.

"Well, I'll go rest for a while," she sighed. "I'm tired. Nice to meet you, Joanie."

"Nice to meet you too, Ruth."

Mike's mother gave me a half smile, and then walked unsteadily down the hall to her bedroom.

There was no anger or rebellion in her; her spirit was broken by circumstance and sickness, a brooding rat that gnawed at her petite frame. The illness was insidious, it would never release her.

Mike's father worked on the bread trucks, delivering bread, but I was curious. I wondered what had happened to his family.

"Your mother was beautiful."

"Yes, she was beautiful. She used to tap dance at the Berkeley Carteret Hotel with her sister, Betty. My mother was a dancer and acrobat. She's Irish—proud and stubborn. She hasn't been feeling well for a long time. I had to learn to wash my own clothes and iron at a young age. My mother fell sick years ago, has trouble walking. My father does most of the cooking. He's a pretty good cook."

I heard the screen door slam.

"Anybody home?"

"Yeah, Dad. Joanie and I, home from school."

"Jimmy's home early," he murmured. "I guess he lost all his money again at the track. He's at the track most of the time. Doesn't win much, though."

I thought of my comfortable home, and how I would sit in front my dressing table, primping for a date and worrying about my makeup. Suddenly, I had knots in my stomach.

"Yup, that's my father, they call him 'Jimmy the Horse.'"

"Jimmy the Horse?"

"Yeah, it's from a movie about a guy who dies and comes back as a racehorse."

"I think I saw that movie once. The man comes back as a racehorse and tells his friends which horses to bet on. It was a funny movie. I forget the ending."

"There's no happy ending."

"So that's it," I thought to myself.

Monmouth Park was a lush, manicured racetrack nestled between the ocean and Highway 35 in Oceanport. Before each race, a bugler, resplendent in red waistcoat and cap, climbed a small tower and played the tune that heralded the start of the race. The horses filed into the starting gate while the crowd quieted in anticipation.

"They'rrr off!" shouted the announcer, as the crowd cheered wildly.

"It's Whirlwind in the lead, followed by Roman Chariot and Jersey Mike. But wait, it's Paddy's Pride coming up the backstretch. It's Paddy's Pride neck and neck with Jersey Mike.

"It's Paddy's Pride taking the rail and heading for the finish line—and it's Paddy's Pride by a head!

"What an upset, folks! Paddy's Pride wins it by a head! A long shot!"

The crowd moaned. One could hear the disgruntled voices of the losers in the background.

"Hold all tickets until the race is declared official."

A few moments of silence.

"It's official. Paddy's Pride is the winner!" boomed the announcer.

The tote board lit up in a flash of colorful numbers. The fans shrugged and paced. Some fans threw their tickets angrily in the air while others hurried to the ticket windows to place their bets. The crowd milled about restlessly, awaiting the next race.

So it went, race after race, day after day. It's not for me to pass judgment on anyone. One man's entertainment is another man's ruin.

Mike's father strode into the kitchen.

"Well, what have we got here?" he exclaimed.

"Dad, this is Joanie, my new girl."

"Joanie, this is my dad."

"Glad to meet you, Mr. Corcione," I chirped like a chickadee.

"Call me Jimmy, little girl."

"OK, Jimmy, nice to meet you."

This informality was new to me.

"Well, you're a very pretty young lady."

Mike put his arm around me. I was embarrassed. This was a new experience. Men were paying attention to *me.* At home, everyone paid attention to my younger brothers. Suddenly, I was the center of attention, and there was no baklava in sight.

The worn linoleum creaked beneath my feet.

"Hey, wanna' stay for dinner?" Mike offered.

I wondered if dinner would be more baloney-and-cheese sandwiches, but I didn't care.

"It's Wednesday—we always send out for pizza on Wednesday."

"Pizza for dinner?"

"Never had pizza for dinner? Well, little girl, it's time you had some good Italian food."

I was accustomed to homemade lamb and avgolemono soup. Mike had beguiled me with his down-to- earth lifestyle. He was a young man with no pretense. Generous for a poor boy.

Suddenly I saw myself as a painted princess—a made-up kewpie doll. I was empty-headed and self-centered. All I thought about were clothes, friends, and boys. I didn't know how to do anything constructive. I was a fake in a fake world.

Mike lived in a different world than mine. His world was one of survival, the world of reality.

"I'll be right back," Mike stated. "I'm going to Freddie's to get a pizza. Keep my father company."

I sat silently at the kitchen table studying my new surroundings. Mike's father reached into an old tin breadbox and grabbed a fresh loaf of Italian bread. Moving quickly, he grabbed a knife and sliced the loaf into uneven chunks.

"I'll be right back," he announced, as he rushed out the back door.

"Now where's he going?" I thought to myself, as the screen door slammed shut.

Jimmy was back in the kitchen within five minutes. His dark, rough hands held three freshly picked tomatoes.

"See these?" he said proudly, "I grew them in my garden with my own hands. You like tomatoes?"

"Oh, yes. I like tomatoes."

Mike's father began slicing the tomatoes. He opened the refrigerator, grabbed a hunk of provolone cheese and a bowl of big green olives, and placed them ceremoniously on the table.

"Do you have a garden?"

"No, but we have a gardener."

"Well, well. A gardener, but no garden? Wait till you try these tomatoes, little girl. Best tomatoes you ever ate," he assured me, grabbing a heavy plate, and arranging the juicy red slices around the edge.

"Olive oil, needs some olive oil," he smiled, drizzling the golden liquid over the slices, and adding some olives on the side.

"Oh yes, wine," he chuckled.

"I forgot the wine."

"Wine?" I cried. "I can't have wine. I'm not old enough."

Jimmy stood perfectly still.

"Why, we always have wine with Italian food! This is homemade wine, straight from my father's cellar!"

He reached over to the shelf, grabbed a carafe, and poured me a small glass of homemade wine.

"Grandpa's wine."

"Here, little girl, have a sip."

I took a tiny sip. The wine was rich and earthy. Then I heard the front door slam.

"Here's the pizza! Wait'll you taste it. Sal made it special—lotsa cheese."

Mike placed the pizza box on the table and grabbed some paper plates. He opened the box and the aroma of freshly baked pizza, dripping with mozzarella cheese, filled the room. I took another sip of wine. The fruity wine mingled with the smell of tomatoes and provolone. Steaming vapors of melted cheese and tangy tomato sauce rose into the air, filling my nostrils with the wonder of Italy. I envisioned gondoliers rowing down the Venetian canals, serenading me with "*O Sole Mio, O Solo Mio*," while I dreamed of Rome and the Coliseum.

Mike cut the first piece of pizza and slid in onto my plate. "Let it cool a minute," he cautioned.

I waited patiently. As the bubbly cheese relaxed, I lifted the luscious masterpiece and took a bite. *Delicioso*! The gondoliers were still singing. I looked at Mike's handsome face and realized that this might be a lifelong romance. As our eyes met, I realized that, for the first time in my life, I was really in love.

I was in love with Italian food.

"Boy, was that great pizza!" Mike proclaimed, as he wiped his mouth on a paper napkin. "Why don't we go out somewhere? How about a walk on the boardwalk?"

"Are you sure your mother is okay?"

"Yeah, sure. She's tough."

"Like you?"

"Yeah, like me. Let's go."

"Well, maybe I better get home. I'm stuffed."

We left the empty box on the table and headed for the front door.

"Nice to meet you, Jimmy," I called out, as Jimmy cleared the table and downed another glass of homemade wine.

Mike led me down the steps and toward the street. I was surprised at how many neighbors stopped to wave and say hello. An old man carrying a long white bag of Italian bread stopped and called out to us.

"That your new girl, Mike? She's cute. Say hello to Jimmy for me."

Well, I wasn't really pretty, but I guess I *could* pass for "cute."

Mike's mother, Ruth, 1940s

"Where have you been?" my father questioned when I returned home. "You missed dinner, we had lamb and rice. Are you hungry?"

"No, I had pizza over Mike's house."

"Pizza? What kind of dinner is that?"

"Italian," I countered.

"Italian?"

Now my father was glaring at me.

"I have to make my own choices, Dad. Nationalities don't matter anymore."

"What do you mean, Joanie? Nationalities *always* matter. Always!"

"You're not helping me with my adolescence," I blurted out as I marched upstairs to my room. "Old- fashioned!"

That's all there was to it. My parents were boring and old-fashioned. I lived in a stuffy world where my mother's weekly routine centered around waxing the furniture and entertaining the garden club ladies.

We spent a lot of time that year walking the boardwalk, going to movies, and listening to music. Mike wanted to be a good buddy, a tough guy, and a lover. On our first Christmas together, he bought me black slacks and a black sweater. I was impressed! Mike and I became inseparable. We walked the streets of Asbury Park without a care in the world. Movies, dancing, and bowling were the main forms of entertainment in the late fifties. We would sit together in the balcony of the Mayfair Theater, munching popcorn and watching the illusion of dreamy white clouds floating across the blue-vaulted ceiling.

Mike and I took long walks together on the beach, listening to the running tide and searching for shooting stars. Our little seashore town was lovely at night. If you stood on the boardwalk, you could count the stars. We could walk anywhere and meet friends. Families were close, storekeepers were respected, and neighbors helped each other. Drugs were for derelicts. Saturday night was for cruising the beachfront.

Car clubs such as the "Haulin' Gents" and the "Motor Jockeys" set the stage for would be hot-rodders. Mike's next car was an old '49 Packard. The front seat was as roomy as a sofa, and the interior smelled like my grandmother's parlor. The radio blasted songs of young love, broken hearts, and betrayals.

We knew all the words to the songs, and each couple had "their song." Our song was "Tonight, Tonight," by the Mello-Kings. Mike taught me how to dance. I was skinny, knock-kneed, and bowlegged, but Mike did this funny step he called the "fish," which I thought was downtown Asbury Park. We danced this step to "Pledging My Love," with lyrics "I'll forever love you the rest of my days; I'll never part from you and your loving ways" that fit perfectly. No more parking and drinking beer, now I was being treated like a princess.

Mike had very little money, so it was a surprise when he took to a fancy restaurant. He got all slicked up in a new gray sharkskin suit that he bought on the advice of his friend, Carl Williams. Carl was a clothing salesman on Springwood Avenue, otherwise known as the "Ave." Years later, Carl became the successful operator of an upscale men's clothing store on Cookman Avenue, a few doors down the street from my father's candy store. Carl was known as "Mr. Fashion." I'll never forget when Carl, dressed in a dark pinstripe suit, gray tie, and wide-brimmed hat, appeared at my husband's wake with his Asbury Park High School yearbook tucked under his arm.

Mike had an amazing knack for making friends and keeping them for life. He collected friends. Sometimes his friend Frankie would drive us around in his red and white Mercury, or Richie would borrow his father's Cadillac, pick up his date, and we'd all head for the local drive-in.

Nationalities didn't matter to Mike, nor did a person's color or where he lived. He had a lot of Italian friends: Johnny Sis, Sammy Yac, and Henry Vaccaro. He also hung around with the King boys, Barry Slott, Warren Rodkin, and Skippy Levinski, and they all played football together. Barry and Warren played a big part in Mike's life. Years later, Barry would help Mike and me out of many, many difficulties. Mike's friends remembered him right up to the end.

10

Although Asbury Park abounded with beauty and charm, the real glory lived and breathed in its smorgasbord of immigrants. Italians, Jews, African Americans, Greeks, Armenians, and Gypsies populated the town. There were English, Irish, Scotch, and Chinese nationalities. Protestant, Baptist, and Methodist churches stood like castles along Lake Avenue.

There were two Jewish synagogues in town. When I was thirteen, I went to four bar mitzvahs. My friends taught me funny words such as *tuchus*, *shmuck*, and *yenta*. They introduced me to bagels and lox, and I introduced them to baklava. I remember playing Spin the Bottle with Lenny Braverman and Larry Wigdortz and sneaking glances at Jeff Phillips. I had a crush on Abbie Marner, my neighbor down the street. My father tolerated these dalliances, as he envisioned me marrying a Greek boy.

Asbury Park had a flourishing African-American community. Its main street, Springwood Avenue, offered an assortment of untapped talent and potential. In grammar school, I was surprised to discover that many of the girls in home economics already knew how to cook and sew. All I knew was how to make toast. I remember schoolmates such as Joe Reed, Faye Peak, Gloria Hartwell, and Elizabeth Budd.

Elizabeth's brother, Frank Budd, was a member of the USA Olympic track team.

Asbury also had a thriving Gypsy community. My father liked the Gypsies because they worked quietly and never complained. Once they repaired the dents in the store's copper pots. Madame Marie was the matriarch of the family. She had olive skin, dark upswept hair, and strong shoulders. There was something mystical about her. She didn't smile much, and turned from your gaze, adding to her intrigue.

Madame Marie had a flair for the theatrical and cultivated this persona. Her crisp white fortune telling stand on the boardwalk was complete with swirls of blue stars and astrological signs. You could hear the clink of jewelry and the sweep of her peasant skirt as her slippers padded over the splintery boards. Whenever a customer entered her booth, Madame Marie's graceful hands parted the brightly beaded curtains and dropped them with a flourish. I longed to sneak into the booth and have my fortune told, but my parents forbid it.

My imagination ran wild. I imagined our dark eyes meeting as Madam Marie traced her fingers across my palm and conjured up my future.

"Ah-h, I see a handsome stranger in your future. He is strong, very strong, very brave, but he will fall, and you will become strong. You will have many children."

Stop right there.

I wondered if fortune tellers could gaze into a crystal ball, or peer into a porcelain cup and reveal the future in wet tea leaves.

Sylvia, a Gypsy girl, was a brief classmate of mine in grammar school. Sylvia was quiet, serene, and polite. I can still picture her thick black hair wrapped about her head in a neat bun and pressed against her golden skin. She, too, carried an air of mystery about her, like a cloud passing over the moon.

Sylvia may have been related to Madame Marie. I always wondered what happened to Sylvia. In those days, many children followed their family's occupations. I wonder if Sylvia become a fortune teller too. I wonder if Madam Marie's booth is still there, adding its mystique to the Asbury boardwalk.

Bruce Springsteen immortalized Madame Marie in his song "The Fourth of July." To me, Bruce Springsteen writes with honesty as he describes the colorful everyday life of ordinary people. One of my favorite Springsteen songs is "Jersey Girl."

Whenever I hear the lyrics, "Down the shore, everything's all right," I get homesick.

That's me, a Jersey girl. Even with all my heartaches, no matter where I go, I'll always be a Jersey girl. I could travel to the ends of the earth, only to compare them to the Jersey Shore. I could travel to the Greek islands and the sands of Egypt, only to dream of the sand and sea of my youth. I could meet new people, but they would only remind me of my old friends. I could journey to different lands and meet people of all nationalities only to be reminded of the diverse ethnicity of the Jersey Shore. I could walk the biggest boardwalk in the world, and still long for the boardwalk of my youth.

I took my hometown for granted. The economy prospered through hard work and a strong community spirit. By the 1950s, Asbury Park had become a bustling center of elegant, colorful shops. Steinbach's, a fashionable department store with elevators, designer clothing, and furniture, was the anchor store of Cookman Avenue. Across the street stood the *Asbury Park Press* building, a stronghold of loyal journalists. Tafsun's shoe store featured glitzy sling backs, spiked heels, and penny loafers. Down from Tafsun's stood the Golden Rule, an upscale clothing store for children.

When I was seventeen, I would walk around the corner from the candy store, stroll over to Main Street and look in the windows of the shops.

One particular shop intrigued me. The heavy iron sign stated "Pawn Shop." The window was a pirate's chest of treasures and castoffs. Ornate rings, glossy pearls, and diamond brooches dozed in black velvet cases, tempting prospective customers. Gold watches and ruby earrings sparkled in the sun. Besides jewelry, there was an eclectic assortment of former possessions: leather bags, suitcases, and a set of pink and white Limoges china.

No matter how meager their appearance, all the castoffs had a story to tell. My eyes scanned the assortment of discarded items. An old manual typewriter, sitting in the corner like a forgotten relative, finally caught my eye. The typewriter looked out of place behind the elegant jewelry and fine china.

The round, glossy keys reminded me of delicate fingers, just waiting to form thoughts. Gold lettering contrasted the black onyx keys, and the high, skeletal carriage signified an air of superiority. The key at the bottom read "Shift" and another read "Back." "Underwood Standard Typewriter" was etched in gold letters at the bottom. I didn't even know how to type, but I was willing to learn. I never had a typewriter, but I knew I had to have this one. I gathered my courage and strode into the store.

The store was dim and smelled like old men's clothes. A faded reproduction of Van Gogh's "Sunflowers" hung crookedly on the wall. An odd assortment of china, lamps, and radios sat haphazardly on the sturdy shelves. Dust particles slid down random shafts of light like tiny cable cars. Behind the counter stood a small, skinny, man. He was probably only middle-aged, but his pale complexion and thinning hair made him look older. I was almost sure that he was the proprietor.

"May I help you, Miss?" he asked in a raspy voice.

I cleared my throat and tried to look older than my seventeen years.

"Yes, I'm interested in that old typewriter in the window." I used the term "old" strategically to get a better price.

"Ah, yes. It's an antique, but it works well. Here, I'll show it to you."

He walked over to the window, lifted the typewriter from its display, and placed it with a thud on the counter. The dust particles swirled furiously, as if in annoyance.

"See, it works fine," he sighed, tapping the keys, *tap, tap, tap*.

Each key was attached to the carriage by a cage of long, black metal arms. It almost seemed as if the typewriter was alive and could think for itself. I wondered what stories the typewriter had to tell. I wondered about the previous owner. What circumstances had forced them to sell such a practical possession? What kind of letters had been written? Were they business letters, sad letters, or love letters?

"How much is the typewriter?" I said with authority.

"Well, this is an *antique.* See the gold lettering? It's an Underwood."

"Hmm-mm," I mused, recognizing the sales pitch.

"There's a price here," he said, flipping a tiny white tag. "Five dollars."

I frowned. "What? Five dollars?"

"Well, it *is* an antique."

"Antique? It isn't an antique. It's just an old typewriter. I really like it, but I only have three dollars right now. Would you take three dollars for it?"

"The price is five dollars."

"That's too much. I don't think the owner is coming back. He must have left town."

"Maybe not."

"How about three dollars?"

"How about five?"

"I only have three."

I tapped the keys randomly.

"The letter '*I*' sticks. Three dollars."

"Young lady, why don't you come back another time?"

"I'm not coming back."

He crossed his arms over his chest.

"Three dollars, that's my final offer."

"What do you want it for?"

"I want to better myself."

"Better yourself?"

"Yes, see my uniform? I'm tired of waiting on customers in my father's store. That's what I do all day, put candy in boxes."

"That's not so bad."

"Did you ever work for Greeks who are your family?"

"I see."

"Well. . . if it makes a young lady happy." He smiled, flapping his loose dentures.

"Three dollars."

I took three crinkled bills out of my wallet and handed him the money. I figured that the typewriter was worth less than the price tag, but the proprietor still made a profit. I carried the typewriter to my car and sat it proudly on the front seat, then drove around the corner to the candy store.

The tiny bell over the front door jingled merrily as I lugged my treasure into the candy store. My father was standing behind the register counting money.

"Where have you been? I have customers waiting! You're always late."

"Look what I bought, Dad," I announced, placing the typewriter on the shelf behind the counter.

"What have you bought now?"

"A typewriter."

He slammed the register door shut with a clang that echoed through the store like the Liberty Bell.

"A typewriter! What do you need a typewriter for? You buy things you don't need, just like your mother! Clothes, shoes. . .."

He grimaced, running his fingers through his dark, wavy hair.

"I need a typewriter."

"A typewriter? What are you going to do with a typewriter? You should be here waiting on customers."

"I don't want to wait on customers. I want to learn to type."

"What? *Type*! Why don't you learn to cook? What are you going to do when you get married?"

"Married? I'm only seventeen! I want to learn to type so I can write stories."

"Write stories! Why should you write stories when you should be learning to cook?"

"I suppose you're still mad because I bought my own car. It's just an old '54 Plymouth, but it runs. I paid for it myself, $150."

"Too much money! I told you! You don't need a car. Women don't need cars. Get your boyfriends to drive you around. Women shouldn't be driving anyway."

"Women?" I whined. "At least my mother doesn't fall asleep at the wheel! Besides, I can't depend on boyfriends!"

"When did I ever fall asleep at the wheel?" he groaned.

"Just about every day!"

"Impossible! You always make things up. You exaggerate just like your mother. Besides, you were supposed to be at work half an hour ago. Where were you?"

"Buying a typewriter."

My father threw his hands up in the air again and went back to putting innocent marshmallows on top of small rounds of caramels. And so it continued, over and over again, marshmallows on top of caramels.

When I brought the typewriter home, I discovered that the key for the letter "I" really did stick.

In summer, I would go down the worn steps to the candy store's cellar and help Dad make ice cream. The cellar was a damp, cool refuge from the summer heat. It was fun to sample the freshly made, soft ice cream. My father would pour fresh cream and sugar into the top of a rotating steel cylinder. I pushed the large plastic bucket underneath the spigot, carefully rotating the ice cream as it swirled into the bottom. Together my father and I lugged the bucket of ice cream across the cellar floor and into the freezer.

One day I asked, "Dad, why don't you just sell soft ice cream? It's so-o good!"

"No, no."

He poured more milk into the top of the cylinder.

"That would never work."

He shook his head. "No one would buy soft ice cream."

You couldn't help but love a man who spent his life making chocolates and ice cream.

11

One of my father's favorite targets was my mother's brother, Uncle Ken. Uncle Ken stood about 6'4". When he walked into a room, he took center stage. I remember him standing in the doorway to Gran's house, his sun-streaked brown hair falling in a soft wave over his forehead, and his blue eyes chasing the shadows away. I'll say this for my mother's family—they were some vibrant, good-looking people. When I was a little girl, I idolized him. He always said that I was from "his side of the family."

Uncle Ken had a 1938 Chevy that he kept in Gran's backyard. It was a sturdy, comfy sedan, with running boards, rusting fenders, and a massive hood. My brother George and I used to hop inside and pretend to drive, until one day Ken locked the car up forever. Uncle Ken was a novelty to us because he worked at Sears and Roebuck. In other words, he had a *real* job. He actually had to take orders from other people, whereas my father simply had his own business. Ken, like my mother, presented himself with the posture and confidence of a member of the royal court. It was obvious that Uncle Ken regarded my Greek relatives as court jesters.

What made Ken unique at the time was that he shared his life with Uncle Fred. They lived two blocks from the beach in a sumptuous apartment overlooking Deal Lake. Ken and Fred made me feel proud to be a little girl. I loved horses, and when I was seven, Ken and Fred bought me a metal hobbyhorse that slid across the floor.

Ken and Fred drove a 1960 white Cadillac complete with bright red leather seats and shiny chrome hubcaps. When my uncle and his friend drove up to our house, my mother would fold her hands in prayer, bring them to her chin, and exclaim: "I hope the neighbors are watching!" Since my father had spent eight hours stirring boiling pots of sticky caramels, lifting hot kettles of chocolate fudge, and scraping marshmallow off the soles of his shoes, he didn't share my mother's enthusiasm for her brother's visits. Ken and Fred used to park their Cadillac at the curb, amble up the walkway, and sit down for coffee. My father would wipe the chocolate off his cuffs, dust the confectioner's sugar from his shirtsleeves, and run a comb through his curly hair. He stifled the frown on his face and welcomed Ken and Fred to the table.

One of the major differences between the families was that my mother's family would sit down to a meal without stabbing choice cuts of meat off the plate of the person seating next to them. Also, my mother's family didn't shout "attack" when they carved the traditional Thanksgiving turkey. My mother cringed at the spectacle of roasting a lamb in the backyard.

Ken and Fred sat quietly while sipping coffee.

"Fred, would you like more lemon chiffon pie?" my mother asked.

"No, Margie, that's fine."

"How about you, Ken?"

"Yes, of course. It's delicious."

My mother would smile and quietly slice through the cool lemony filling down to the homemade graham-cracker crust, then gently slip the piece onto her favorite Limoges dessert plate.

Ken quietly stirred his coffee.

"Our mother's china looks lovely in your house, Margie. The pattern matches perfectly."

"Uh, Margie," my father interrupted, "I'd like some more pie, too. The pie is very good, but bring me another cup of coffee—none of those fancy cups either."

At least both sides of the family agreed on one thing. They loved my mother's pies. This just proves that a good pie has more power in some social situations than a well-turned phrase. It's also interesting how my father's attitude improved when food was served.

I'll never forget the first time we visited Ken and Fred's apartment. My father agreed to drive us to this cultural adventure, even though he tried to use the excuse that he had to make caramel apples that afternoon. I was about twelve at the time, and my brothers were about nine and three. My mother was always gushing over them, while I was considered a great burden to the family because I was a girl.

Dad drove us over the rickety bridge that connected Interlaken to Asbury Park. The dark gray waters of Deal Lake lapped gently against the concrete seawall as the salty ocean air flooded our nostrils.

The yard was manicured. Just as we approached the front door and were about to knock, Fred opened the door with a flourish. (Fred was the master of the flourish.) My father's eyes widened as Fred stood before us, dressed conservatively, but wearing a red ruffled apron.

"Margie, Angy, Joanie! So good to see you! Welcome!" he gushed. "I just baked a cake."

Ken stepped boldly to the door and added, "Fred bakes good cakes. He's a wonderful cook. Come in, we'll show you around."

Our eyes took in the apartment all at once. Our home was lovely, but Ken and Fred's apartment shone like a palace. Large blocks of undulating glass framed the foyer, and the living room was resplendent with gilt-framed paintings and marble tables. An antique china cabinet displayed Ken and Fred's collection of ivory figurines. A scenic picture window framed a panoramic view of the sparkling lake. Even my father was in awe. As we wandered into the next room, the kitchen and dining room expanded before us. The den was a bastion of tranquility, and as we stepped down, the lower level dipped down before us.

Suddenly we heard what sounded like a baby crying. Even though I was dulled by the childhood stupor of naiveté, I could not explain this phenomenon, unless some young woman had left a baby on the doorstep. The explanation was simple. There, slinking around the corner of the den was a strikingly beautiful Siamese cat. Her blue eyes widened at our intrusion, and she stopped, studying us for a moment, then quickly skittered away in a blur of beige fur.

"Oh, that's just Duchess, our Siamese," Ken chuckled. "She has a distinctive meow."

"She certainly does," cracked my father. My father tolerated cats, but he never liked dogs. Naturally, dogs loved him because he always smelled like sugar, chocolate, and evaporated milk. Dogs would jump up and lick his face affectionately, but he would nudge them away only to have them sit on his shoes and lick his hands.

"What a gorgeous cat!" Mother gushed.

"Yes, she's beautiful!" I chimed in.

"Where's the bathroom?" my father asked, dusting confectioners' sugar off his shirtsleeves.

"Oh, we have two. I'll show you to the one by the living room," Fred replied modestly. "Hope you like the mink doorknobs," he laughed.

"Mink doorknobs?" my father responded sarcastically.

"Yes, they *do* add an extra touch to the décor, don't you think?" Fred asked in all sincerity.

Mink doorknobs? This was irresistible. My family just had to see these furry creations. We took turns sneaking down the hall to the bathroom just to see the mink doorknobs. Lo and behold, there they were, as brown and furry as the Siamese cat. I guess Ken and Fred chose their bathroom décor to match the cat. The doorknob covers were real mink—soft and silky. All we talked about on the drive home were the mink doorknobs. My father was miserable.

Ken and Fred were warm and friendly, but I'll never forget my Uncle Wilbur and Aunt Julie. They were a loving, down-to-earth couple who were always on the go. They were just plain happy. On summer weekends, when the sun warmed the shore, Wilbur and Julie would pack up their car and make the long drive from Clifton to their Point Pleasant home. Wilbur had a shock of premature white hair that fell in a wave over his tanned brow. He would stand on the beach, cup his hands, and echo his Viking call over the water.

Aunt Julie was a stunning brunette with sparkling sapphire eyes and a talent for baking deep-dish pies. Wilbur and Julie had three rambunctious boys: Ricky, Robert, and Billy. The boys would often spend a few weeks in July at Gran's house in Bradley Beach. We held our noses at the stinky carton of worms in the fridge, but as long as the boys loved the ocean, they could do no wrong. Our dinners revolved around Chef Boyardee pasta, hotdogs, and tomato sandwiches, but it was the best time of my life.

My cousins were my idols—their sense of daring fascinated me. Gran never said a word when the boys took the radio apart to see how it worked. They would scatter all the parts over the dining room table, but in an hour, they had magically reassembled the entire radio. Since my father's mechanical ability consisted of turning on the marshmallow machine, my cousin's skills amazed me.

Point Pleasant Beach was a sleepy fishing town complete with a boardwalk, rides, and a deep inlet to the ocean. Lumbering fishing boats braved the powerful currents that flowed between the gray boulders, as fishermen tossed their lines into the uncertain current. The salt spray crashed upon the rocks, flinging the sea into the sky. A shout goes up, a pole bends, and a shimmering fish emerges from the deep. The fisherman proudly reels in the fish, unhooks it, and tosses it into a white pail where it flops helplessly. Curious bystanders amble over to the pail, peer inside, and study the hapless catch.

People are like that—just plain curious. It's amazing how easily people are entertained. Onlookers would stop and stare at the flapping fish as if it were a rock star. To the fish, it was the wrath of Poseidon. The fishermen went back to the water. The gawkers moved on and all was forgotten.

In the summer, the breezes were cool and balmy, and the whole town smelled of salt air and dead fish. While July and August were soft and gentle, the winters were fierce and bitter. In winter, biting cold winds whipped the waves into a raging cauldron, as the fishing boats pitched and fell in the dangerous troughs. Still, the fishermen braved the elements, and many lost their lives. Today there is a statue by the Manasquan inlet in commemoration of the dedicated fishermen who spend their lives, and often lose them, on the sea. Hurricanes and nor'easters were the bane of the Jersey Shore. Storms tore up the boardwalk like matchsticks, washed away entire beaches, but the Jersey Shore people remained undaunted, rebuilding the damage and our lives.

There is a timeless ebb and flow of life at the Jersey Shore that churns and lulls us like the changing of the tide. We persevere through the hardships because we know that summer will come again, year after year, and that each endless summer makes all the storms bearable. Sometimes we burned to a crisp in the August sun. Our skin would peel off in little white rings in a few days, but my stoic cousins never complained, so I, too, suffered in silence. I tried not to chicken out as I braved the highest waves or flinch when I threaded a wriggling worm on a hook. On cool days we searched the jetty for trapped sea life. Sometimes we liberated the tiny crustaceans that gasped for life in the mossy crevices.

Wilbur and Julie had a motorboat that they kept at their Point Pleasant bungalow, and they often invited us for a boat ride. My father would drive up in his shiny black Chrysler with my mother, brothers, and me arranged in our respective seats.

"Hi there, Angy," Wilbur called out, "why are you wearing a suit? Don't you want to go out on the boat?"

"Not really, Wilbur," he shrugged. "I spent enough time on a boat when I was in the Navy."

"Come in! We just caught some nice flounder. We're cleaning them up right now," exclaimed Uncle Wilbur, scraping fish scales into the air.

"Please stay for dinner," Aunt Julie insisted.

"Oh, yes, we'd love to," my mother smiled sweetly. "Wouldn't we, Angy?"

"Yes, yes, Mah-gie," he fibbed. "I'd love to," he lied.

"C'mon Angy, how about a dip in the river?" Uncle Wilbur asked. He turned toward a hook on the wall and announced, "Here, I have some extra bathing suits."

My father looked at Uncle Wilbur as if he had just offered him a root canal. "No thanks, I hate sand."

His eyes scanned the room. Uncle Wilbur turned toward the cutting board and continued cleaning bluefish. Tippy the dog was yapping wildly, and there was fresh bait on the counter. Wilbur and the three boys were all in their bare feet. It was so inviting that I wanted to kick off my shoes and become part of the family.

There were no Greek tragedies—no philosophy. Wilbur and Julie and the boys were just an average family enjoying a weekend at their bungalow by the beach. These people were everything I wanted to be, close to nature and to each other. This was a family that really knew how to enjoy life! For them, life was an adventure. My cousins took turns motoring us around the Manasquan River. My clothes were wet with salt spray, and my hair turned bronze in the sun.

We shared a wonderful dinner of baked flounder, corn, and blueberry pie.

"Julie," my father exclaimed as a smile spread over his face, "This pie is excellent!" His olive skin brightened as he wiped away an errant blueberry.

My mother reached over and hugged him. She was proud of him and her family, too. So was I. How I admired my mother's family. I wanted to be just like them.

On the way home my father murmured: "I just don't know about your family: Why do they go barefoot?"

12

Not only did Asbury Park feature a steamy Chinese laundry where my father brought his shirts, it also had an upscale Chinese restaurant. The restaurant was located above a swank men's store near the railway. Our parents often took us there for dinner. We climbed the steep stairs, and the hostess seated us at a table complete with a crisp white tablecloth and folded linen napkins. A slender waiter took our order then, silently filled our tiny cups with hot Chinese tea. The red and black décor was so compelling that we could hardly concentrate on our dinner. I was surprised to learn that the local Greek men gathered at the Chinese restaurant in the afternoons to play Greek rummy.

We were a family then. Some Sundays we took long rides in the country. My father would sing to us in his deep voice—sometimes a Greek song, sometimes a hit song such as "You Gotta' Have Heart," from the show "Damn Yankees."

I don't know why, but whenever he sang the Irish song, "I'll Take You Home Again, Kathleen," I got a lump in my throat. It was a beautiful song about a girl who was homesick for her Irish homeland. Even today, the song chokes me up.

In late spring our father would drive us all to the boardwalk. The Arcade boasted an antique carousel inhabited by fanciful animals plunging headlong in an endless race. In spring, when the weather-beaten bronze doors were flung open, the strains of the Wurlitzer boomed, "East side, west side, all around the town," across the lake. My father sat on the verdigris bench and marveled at the mythological menagerie of lions, tigers, and sea serpents twirling by.

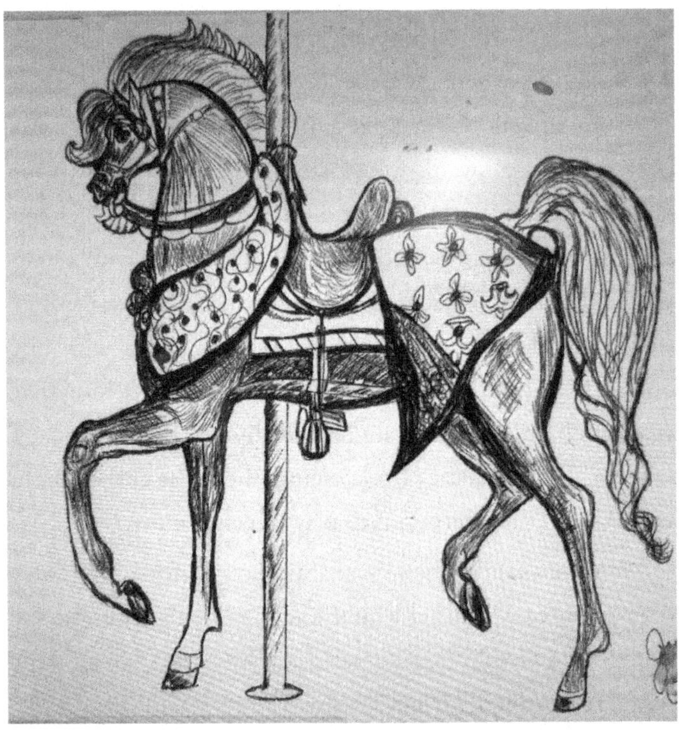

Asbury Park was a town of movers and shakers. Like the carousel, we were always in motion. I can still hear the creaking of the old porch swing as it rocked back and forth like a cradle. Sometimes the grating sound of the traveling knife sharpener shattered the silence of the neighborhood.

Mr. Petro, our gardener, kept our lawn lush and green. Even though my father couldn't grow a petunia, he insisted on telling Mr. Petro what work he wanted done. Mr. Petro would patiently listen and make tactful suggestions. Thankfully, Mr. Petro's expertise won out. The lawn always looked neat and trimmed. That was the time before landscaping companies, with their ear-splitting equipment, became popular. It was the time of one man, one mower.

It was fall. The violets and lilies of the valley had shed their dainty flowers months ago, the morning glories were fading on the vine. Fall was the harbinger of bonfires and crisp winter mornings. I remember my father and Mr. Petro standing beneath the red maple tree. The grass was thinning, and the trees were ablaze with orange and gold. Mr. Petro would gesture to my father, lean over and run his hands through the grass. My father nodded in agreement, pretending to understand.

I never knew what they were saying, but it didn't matter. What I *did* understand was the mutual respect that my father and Mr. Petro had for one another. They loved to work with their hands and weren't afraid to get them dirty. Each man worked hard, was his own boss, and a successful businessman in his own right.

For my father, autumn meant preparing for Thanksgiving and Christmas. It was time for creating the colors of Christmas, a time to unpack candy canes, and chop sizzling ropes of cinnamon candy into plump squares.

For Mr. Petro, autumn was a time for raking up the crinkled leaves of summer. It was a time for cutting back and replenishing the soil for the next season. Fall was the time to clean machinery, put away tools, and make repairs. It was time for Mr. Petro to move inside and reflect on another job well done.

One man was a gardener, and one man was a candy maker, but the lives of both men were intertwined like ivy on a vine. They lived by the seasons and dedicated their lives to their work, but neither of them knew much about the other's business. Both men are gone now, but I remember them standing together under the maple tree, watching summer fade away.

13

My parents didn't know the twist of fate that would threaten our family. My father valued his business, his family, and the Greek community. My mother valued one thing before all others—her home. I never understood her obsession until she told me the real story of her childhood. Her aristocratic upbringing was a pretense. Everything had been a lie.

Mother was the youngest of four children. In later years, she told me how much her childhood poverty had affected her life. When she was young, her clothes reeked so much of the family's old coal stove that children rubbed their noses when she walked by.

I am convinced that my mother's family tree blossomed with brilliance. Her family came to America from Holland in 1673; they fought in the Revolution and the Civil War. Not only was her family bright, strong, and ambitious, they persevered in the face of adversity. Nothing could hold them down or defeat them. They had good health and good looks.

My mother was no exception. Her clothes were stylish, and her grooming impeccable. Although her closets were small, they were jammed with chiffon, taffeta, and cashmere fashions. Fine lingerie slumbered in white-tissue sleeping bags, inhaling the aroma of rose sachets. Braided hatboxes stood ceremoniously on shelves, awaiting the next fashion show.

I remember a color photograph of my mother dressed as a harem girl and draped in gold lame'. My parents had won first prize that night at a costume party. Naturally, my father was dressed as a sheik, complete with white robe and headdress.

One item of haute couture my mother didn't have was a mink coat, but that would materialize later. Instead, she had a furry mink collar that was quite the style, but to me it was a frightful rag. The minks were sewn together, head to tail, as if they were chasing each other. Although they were dead, the glassy-eyed minks seemed to glare at me while their tiny black feet seemed to claw at my guts like the fox in a fable.

Fate played a large part in my life. Remember the song "I found a million-dollar baby (in a five and ten cent store)"?

One day, my mother and her friend Eileen were walking down Cookman Avenue together. Mother was seventeen and she needed a job. She turned to Eileen and announced: "See this candy store? I'm going inside and get a job. Watch me!"

Well, she got the job. She also fell in love with the boss. Maybe she fell in love with the candy. I wonder what made her stop in front of the candy store and make the decision that changed her life and gave breath to mine. Somewhere I have a black and white photograph of my mother as she stood in front of the candy store. She was about twenty years old and tall in her chunky 1940s heels. She smiled radiantly as her dark blonde hair flowed in the breeze. A striped awning in the background announced "Caramel Shop Candies" in white letters.

That's the way small towns were then, little shops with striped awnings and proprietors who knew your name and family. I love small towns. One of my favorite small towns is my mother's birthplace, the tiny Victorian town of Ocean Grove. In those days, doctors made house calls, and most babies were born at home.

It was just after Thanksgiving in 1921 when the doctor came to the house, looked my grandmother in the eye and said, "Now, Aimee, you better not call me on Christmas Day and tell me you're ready to have this baby!"

To the doctor's dismay, Gran sent for him on Christmas day and my mother was born in the bedroom.

My mother's birthplace is still there, tucked away beside the lake. It's just a gray, nondescript home with a sagging, wrap-around porch. If Gran hadn't insisted on selling that house and moving away from the ominous lake, maybe our family history would have been different.

I always wanted to drive over to the house, walk up the stairs, and knock on the door.

The door would open. The lady of the house would tilt her head and give me a quizzical look.

"Hello, may I come in?" I would flash her my best smile. "My mother was born here. I'd like to see where her life and mine began."

Instead, my courage fades, I slow down and keep going.

What is it that keeps me from stopping and visiting my mother's birthplace? Someday, I'll knock on the door and see where my mother was born. Someday.

14

There are many theories about schizophrenia. Some studies suggest poor nutrition in the womb, some suggest dietary and neurological deficiencies, and some conclude that schizophrenia is hereditary. This is not encouraging news to me. Researchers may never know the cause of schizophrenia. Nonetheless, I keep looking for answers to my mother's illness.

Early photos of my mother as a girl portray her as a happy young woman—athletic, adventurous, and innocent. One of my favorite photos is the photo of my teen mother and her friends laughing and holding hands as they splash through the waves and emerge from the ocean. They are free and one with the sea.

In another photo, my mother is peering over the handlebars of her bicycle as her scrappy, feisty wire-hair terrier, Powers, sits anxiously in the basket. Powers, who was named after mother's movie idol, Tyrone Power, got into a lot of fights. Still, he was her favorite dog.

I wish I could have known my mother when she was young. I wish I could have known her when she was poor and had no shoes. I wish I could have been at the train station as she waved goodbye to her brother Ken, as he pressed his chiseled face against the window and waved back, leaving to serve in the war.

In essence, I wish my mother didn't have a nervous breakdown. Somewhere along the way, this carefree young woman disappeared. In her place was an imposter. The woman in the photos was gone forever; someone had replaced her with a woman who had forgotten to be herself.

"Loving a man can make you crazy," Mother told me. Maybe she was right. Maybe loving anyone can make you crazy.

I guess I loved my grandmother then more than anyone else in the family, even my father. Gran had tremendous energy and health. In summer, she grew as tan and brown as an Indian. With her white suit and high cheekbones, she resembled a Palm Beach aristocrat.

Gran was an accomplished cook. Homemade bread, pies, and apple dumplings popped magically out of the oven. One of her greatest attributes was her irrepressible sense of humor. She quoted literature, read the news, and played the piano. I tried to be as witty as my grandmother, but she was just too quick for me.

When Gran was ninety-three-years old and briefly hospitalized, the nurse asked her: "Aimee, did you move your bowels today?"

Not missing a beat, Gran replied, "No, they're in the same place they were yesterday."

I never saw Gran take a nap, even after we trekked four blocks down to the beach and back. Together we would lug an assortment of beach chairs, water, and sandwiches down to the shoreline. Bradley Beach offered an expansive beach and a small, moss-covered jetty. Rough boulders barricaded the street and shielded us from the wind. During the furious nor'easters, angry waves lashed against the boulders, entangling the remains of crabs, sea robins, and puffer fish in the rocks.

When I was ten, one of my greatest treasures was a petrified seahorse that I found between the boulders. I turned the seahorse over in my hand, examining its delicate features. The seahorse was only about three inches long, but it was well preserved. I could still distinguish the indentations and empty eye sockets. The tiny tail still gripped the dried reeds giving the illusion that the fragile body would magically come to life.

I said a prayer over the seahorse, then placed it in a plastic pail and brought it home. What catastrophe had washed it so far from the sea? Wincing at the destructible power of nature, I wondered how such a delicate creature met such a calamitous end.

In many ways I had an idyllic childhood. Today, on hot summer days, when I hear the song, "Summertime," I think of my childhood.

> Summertime and the livin' is easy.
>
> Fish are jumpin', and the cotton is high.
>
> Your Daddy's rich, and your mama's good
> lookin'; so hush little baby, don't you cry. . .

I did cry—many tears. It's agonizing to have everything and then lose it. Even worse, it seemed to happen overnight.

Gran guarded the family secrets. When I was eighteen, Gran and I sensed that something was wrong. My mother became nervous and anxious about her weight. She became short-tempered, and her once natural smile seemed forced. At home, she lashed out angrily at both of us. I grew fearful of what was happening to her, and to me, too.

Our house was always lively with company. My father's family visited from Lowell, and my mother's family visited from Clifton. My mother's relatives were bright and a lot of fun, while my father's family ate food every hour.

Uncle Wilbur and Aunt Julie were my favorite aunt and uncle. Even after my mother became ill, Wilbur and Julie were always wonderful to me. When my mother had her nervous breakdown, it broke her family's hearts as well as ours.

15

I wonder what compulsion drives us to share our lives with others. I believe that we are more than a species; we are flesh, but we are spirits, too, grasping at the longings of our souls. I have traveled far away from my roots and my culture.

Socrates once said, "I am not a citizen of Greece or Athens, but of the whole world."

Did you ever wonder what your ancestors were really like? I wish I had known my grandfather John better, but he lived in Massachusetts, and I grew up at the Jersey Shore. *Papou* was a strong, hardworking man who had a successful marriage, managed a profitable bakery business, and raised nine children. What more could a man ask for in life?

He was a big man with red hair and green eyes. I remember him smiling at me as he slipped plump loaves of bread onto long wooden pallets, then slid them into the red-brick oven. The smell of freshly baked bread rose from the fire and floated in the air.

Now that I'm older, and most of my life is behind me, I've developed a genuine reverence for my ancestors. There is so little personal satisfaction in today's world.

Many years ago, my father's family sent me a family photo of my grandparents and six of their nine children. The photo was accompanied by an interesting history of the family. The camera had captured a family frozen in time. The photo was probably taken around 1920, when my father was only twelve years old.

As I look into the photo, my ancestors seem to be looking right back at me. John, my grandfather, sits to the right, while my grandmother, Anastasia, sits to his left. My Aunt Helen, her dark hair tumbling to her waist, is surrounded by her five brothers and her cousin Effie. What's fascinating is that everyone looks so contented, except for my father, who looks miserable. Yia-Yia must have been a tireless worker who devoted herself to her family and her two nieces, Effie and Fifi.

My eyes are drawn to the left side of the photo, or, perhaps, my grandmother's eyes draw me there. Yes, there is a resemblance. She was less than five feet tall. As I study the photograph, I see that my grandmother and I share the same, almost mismatched, brown eyes—inquisitive and kind eyes. Each of my grandparents holds a baby on their lap. One baby looks contented, the other is laughing. Not only does Yia-Yia have the same soft face as mine, she wears the same bewildered expression. Her eyes seem to say: "What am I doing here?"

Each family member is dressed in clean, pressed clothes. Every Monday, Yia-Yia boiled the laundry in a huge pot on an old coal stove, and on Tuesday, she and her nieces did all the ironing.

My eyes studied the old photograph and the soft sepia images that once beheld a different world. The image spoke to me of an ancestor from long ago—my grandmother. Her photograph is a vision of a quiet, determined woman.

I ask myself, "Who are you, Anastasia? What part of you lives within me?" The strong meter of an ancient lyric lingered in her slight smile. My grandmother's eyes triumphed with the glory that once was Greece. Although she was only in her late twenties, the careful coaxing of her wavy hair formed an oval around her face, making her appear more sophisticated than she really was. My grandmother became a picture within a picture. The serenity of her dark dress faded into the background and mingled with the rich Persian carpet. Except for the exquisitely delicate lace collar and shiny gold chain that graced her square shoulders, my grandmother was plain and unadorned.

Her name was Anastasia. She was my father's mother. If it hadn't been for Anastasia, and her courage to come to America, I wouldn't exist. I wouldn't be an American. I am proud to say that my grandmother was an immigrant. I am also proud to say that my father was an immigrant, too. To me, they personified the strong, ambitious individuals who formed the essence of our country.

In 1911, Anastasia made the decision to join her husband in America. This was totally against her principles. When she married John, she made him promise not to force her to leave Greece. What happened in those years to change her mind?

I am proud to say that she came of her own free will.

My grandmother's father and brother were Orthodox priests. I can picture my great-grandfather, standing at the altar of his little church in Lagadia, his white robes clouded in incense, leading the congregation in singing *Christos Anesti.*

Many Europeans believed America's streets were "paved with gold." When Anastasia left for America, she turned to look at the dirt floor of her whitewashed mountain home for the last time. As she gathered her two little children around her long skirt, she felt a pang of heaviness in her heart. Faint tears fell from her dark eyes and floated like petals on the blue windflowers that struggled in the rocky soil.

Anastasia sighed as she stood by her door, gathering her children in her arms. She made the sign of the cross, realizing that she may never see her homeland again. There was no need to lock the door. Once she left Greece, she may never return.

Family and friends readied the donkey and cart for her descent down the rocky terrain of the little town. It must have been a hard trek for a young woman with two small children.

Soon Anastasia's eyes squinted beneath the brilliant sun of Piraeus. The uncertainty in her eyes reflected the turbulent wine dark sea of Homer—the sea of Sirens and Odysseus. This was no romantic journey, just a crowded deck marked "Steerage." Her journey would lead her away from her mythical Ithaca—to America.

Poseidon tossed the boat mercilessly. My father was only three years old, and his sister Helen was just a baby. Anastasia was seasick, and her baby daughter wailed loudly. The passengers in steerage were less than understanding and shouted: "Throw the baby overboard! Throw the baby overboard!" Anastasia kept her composure and gripped her children closer.

After many weeks at sea, Anastasia's eyes widened in wonder as the crowded boat sailed beside her new goddess, not a goddess of myth, but a goddess of liberty. The Statue of Liberty was a vision she would remember all her life. The excitement of this bustling land intrigued her. Anastasia would follow her husband to the cold corner of New England. The gutsy immigrants of the Greek ghetto welcomed her as one of their own. On cold winter evenings, when the searing embers of the coal stove burned low before her eyes, she longed for the blue skies of her ancestral home.

My grandmother never returned to her homeland. Anastasia became assimilated with the new wave of immigrants. She bore my grandfather seven more children. Her family prospered in the realization that America was a land of opportunity. Even though she never felt comfortable with the English language, America became her home.

Today, as I search the old photo and look beyond my grandmother's solemn dress, her strength, and her subdued pride, I wonder what it was like when she saw America for the first time. Her eyes are my eyes, her spirit is my spirit. Her new homeland became mine.

16

Interlaken, the town where I grew up, was a sleepy town of graceful oaks and old homes. Our neighbor, Dr. Parry, lived in an impressive English Tudor home that seemed to rise out of the rolling lawn. The doctor was an outgoing, athletic man who loved nature and animals. Every winter, he'd race his wooden iceboat along the frozen lake, and in summer he'd pick wild blackberries in the woods. Dr. Parry built a wooden bridge across the tiny brook beside the house, and a rock-rimmed goldfish pond beside the lake. Pal, his old three-legged dog, followed him everywhere.

The Millar family lived across from our house, next to Dr. Parry. The Millars, much to the chagrin of my father, had two big, friendly dogs wandering around their property. The house featured a white stucco exterior that shaded the circular driveway, as if awaiting the arrival of a coach and four. Black shutters glared condescendingly at intruders, but a tranquil cove peeked out reassuringly from beneath an old weeping willow. Beyond the willow was a damp, overgrown path. The path ran along a grassy riverbank, sloping down to a weathered dock that floated on the bottle green water. The rickety dock seemed to echo with the laughter of childhood.

I knew the path well. It would lead me past the dock, up the steep bank, and beside the overgrown tennis courts. Once beyond the courts, I could glimpse the tranquil lake and continue on, tripping over the knotty roots of twisted oaks, until I reached my secret hideaway.

The playhouse was a hand-built replica of a rustic cottage. The house was located on Dr. Parry's lakefront property, but both families shared the playhouse. The original owners were friends who built the dollhouse for their children to enjoy. Although their children had grown up and moved away, the families graciously allowed the neighborhood children to play on their property.

The dollhouse was one of the sanctuaries of my childhood. Whenever I'm sad, I visualize the dollhouse and think of better times. I was only nine when I visited the dollhouse for the first time. It was as though all my childhood dreams were suddenly revealed. I really hadn't discovered the dollhouse at all. It had always been there, hidden in my subconscious.

I know the dollhouse was real, and not just a figment of my imagination. A few years ago, I visited it again. After I met John, the new homeowner, I told him about the dollhouse in the woods, and how I used to play there when I was a little girl. John smiled and asked me if I would like to take a tour of the property. He led me to a freshly cleared path that wound about the lake. Suddenly, the dollhouse appeared, just the same as I remembered it, even after all these years. I was amazed. John had been restoring the paint and crumbling chimney.

I felt a lump well up in my throat. Through the years, I had visited the dollhouse in memory, but on that day, I visited it again in person. Once the shingles had been painted white, but over the years the paint had become gray and chipped by the wind. Years ago, I used to sneak around the back and see if there were any baby rabbits hiding behind the house. I lured the bunnies out of their burrow by feeding them pieces of white bread soaked in milk.

One morning, our cat caught one of the bunnies and placed it on our front steps as an offering. I immersed myself in childhood tears until Gran explained how life is full of unexplained tragedies.

When I was a young girl, I followed a ritual each time I visited the dollhouse. The front door welcomed me like a benevolent grandparent. Perhaps grandma's hair had faded, and her clothing was out of date, but she still had a story to tell.

I wondered when the dollhouse had been created. I vaguely remembered the Millar children as they were much older than me. Sometimes I lingered by the front latch, then ceremoniously opened the door. The well-worn wooden steps creaked beneath my feet as I hesitated on the threshold. The brass doorknob felt cold and dull against my hand. As I pushed the rusted lock aside, the door eased open. It was never locked.

The rusty hinge squeaked softly in the breeze. As I gently opened the door, I could hear the rustle of field mice scurrying into their nests. I wiped my feet on the braided rug, held my breath, and entered the room. The air was heavy with the scent of old books and worn floorboards. The dust settled at my feet.

My eyes swept across the room as if I were an intruder in some domestic utopia. To my right stood a rustic stone fireplace framed by a gray slate mantel. On the mantel were various knick-knacks and clay sculptures, childhood crafts formed by rolling out bits of clay and twisting them into shapes. China, glassware, and bric-a-brac lined the shelves. The room smelled like old roses, crumpled between the pages of forgotten books.

The room was a shrine to innocence. In the middle of the room, a ceramic tea set graced a small worn table. The teapot stood quietly, waiting for little girl spirits to pour tea. Each time I visited the dollhouse, I made a new discovery. Once, I realized that all the china was mismatched. No two plates were alike. I gingerly picked up a teacup and mismatched saucer, turning them over like a family heirloom. The floor creaked as I picked up a gold-rimmed dinner plate and turned it over in my hand. For an instant I was tempted to take the plate home as a souvenir, but instead, I solemnly returned it to its place on the shelf. I had to leave the dollhouse the way I found it.

To my left was a small, wooden ladder. It had been painted a soft yellow. The ladder led to the loft and was attached to the wall. I climbed up the ladder and peered out through the tiny window that framed the tranquil lake. Sometimes I lingered by the window, hoping to see a vision of my future, but no vision ever came.

Soon the claustrophobic loft closed in on me, and I clambered down the ladder and plopped my feet on the planked floor. The sun was fading to a misty gray and shadows crept along the walls and across the door. The hardwood floor had dulled to a drab brown. Soon the air would grow cold, and the lake would shimmer with ice.

I heard my friend Bonnie calling me. It was getting late. I slammed the door behind me and raced down the path. The sound resonated over the lake until it mingled with the earth and sky, disappearing into the land of lost echoes. A chipmunk scampered into the brush while a ground squirrel eyed me suspiciously. I ran home and didn't look back.

In a few quick years, I would be a teenager and the dollhouse a memory. A new generation of children would discover my hideaway. The old neighborhood would be gone. The street where I played with Bonnie, Gregory, and Penny would belong to a new group of playmates. Although the dollhouse would become a memory, the memory stirred something in my young girl's heart. I knew I would return in spirit, time and time again, to the mystery of womanhood.

The dollhouse lives in the psyche of many a little girl. All the dreams of girlhood—of marriage, motherhood, and family—were locked up in that house. Someday, I, too, would be grown and have my own home, the mythic repository of all that is woman. I wished that someday I would have a daughter, and she would have her own dollhouse, just like this one. I ran my fingers through my hair and dreamed of having a little girl. I would grow out my tomboy cut and braid her hair into mine in a never-ending circle of life. Little did I realize the joy, sadness, and trials that lay ahead.

I wandered, in my mind, through the dollhouse in the woods. I daydreamed of climbing the ladder and gazing across the lake. I found myself wondering if that old boathouse, and the old dock, were there.

Over the years, on cold days, I found myself wondering if the pond had frozen over. I wondered where my childhood friends had gone—we had lost touch through the years. My friends had moved away and were replaced by a new neighborhood gang. I couldn't picture these new strangers, these invaders of my territory, but I could hear them shouting and laughing as they skated on the icy cove. I was happy for them, but sometimes sorrow struck me like a cup of bitter tea.

17

I was fifteen and very self-conscious of my family. My mother was one of the featured singers in a musical at the local Woman's Club. She had chosen to sing the song "Won't You Come Home Bill Bailey?" With her fair skin, blonde hair and blue-brimmed chapeau, she floated like a Southern belle amidst an audience of suitors. I folded my hands and hoped Mother wouldn't embarrass us or herself. Instead, her voice was clear and steady.

> Won't you come home Bill Bailey,
>
> won't you come home,
>
> I'll do the cookin' honey, I'll pay the rent,
>
> I know I done you wrong. . ..

I never heard my mother sing at home, and I was surprised at the clearness of her voice. It was sweet and gentle, but it had a note of sadness in it. I thought to myself: "My mother really has talent!" No wonder she loved musicals such as "Showboat" and "Pocketful of Miracles." She twirled her white lace parasol up and down the stage, as she sang the refrain:

"I know I'm to blame, but ain't it a shame, Bill Bailey won't you please come home," she pleaded, giving her parasol a final twirl.

We all joined the audience in applauding loudly. Mother smiled and curtsied gracefully. She was so happy! I sighed with relief, but my pride turned into puzzlement—my brothers were giggling. But I was proud of my mother. It took nerve to get on stage and sing the leading song. My mother wasn't even nervous. She had the bearing of an actress. Even my father applauded loudly.

I wondered why my mother spent so much time catering to ungrateful kids and a demanding husband? Did she secretly dream of being an actress? What were her childhood dreams?

I didn't know it at the time, but Mother's father had abandoned her when she was five years old, and she still bore the hidden scars. When I look back, I wonder about that song. Now I understand why she sang the lyrics so well. At the time I thought it was a dumb song, but maybe the song held a deeper meaning. Thinking about it now, the words to "Bill Bailey" may have had a double meaning.

Maybe Mother felt trapped by marriage and motherhood. Three years later, I recalled a haunting episode just before my mother had her nervous breakdown. It was a foreshadowing of events to come. She was standing beside the upstairs bathroom window, and I was standing in the corner of the hallway. She had her back to me and didn't see me in the doorway. Mother had pulled her white Battenberg lace curtains aside. The street was empty. It was an idyllic spring day. Her beloved crimson azaleas were in bloom, and the red leaves of her favorite Japanese maple tree rustled in the breeze.

Suddenly, Mother threw her hands over her eyes, as if blocking out the sun, clenched her fists, and cried: "I want to escape this prison! I want to escape! Escape!"

The cry frightened me. "Why was my mother talking like this?" I asked myself. It didn't make sense. My mother always loved the house, as much as life itself. It was almost as if she drew her strength from the very timbers. Now she considered her house a "prison."

It was strange how she began avoiding the large glass mirror that framed the dining room. No longer did she linger in front of her reflection; she quickly walked by. Dust settled on her prized china cabinet and tarnish crept into the crevices of her antique silver set. The home she had meticulously furnished and decorated had become her tomb. Her treasures embellished her sarcophagus.

It was as though my mother didn't notice herself or her surroundings. She didn't even notice me. I wasn't there. Our mother was shutting all of us out of her life. I never said a word. I quietly slunk away, wondering what was happening to our family. Years later, my mother would suffer from agoraphobia, fear of the outdoors, and her house, in a sense, became a prison. I have visions of my mother hiding in a closet after she hadn't eaten for days. Gradually, she lost all her teeth from neglect. Twenty years later, she slipped into a diabetic coma. Diabetes? Where did that come from? I wonder how long she had been a diabetic. I remembered how she lost a lot of weight before she had her breakdown. Our old home movies show a thin, drawn woman where once a shapely, robust woman had been. Why didn't the doctors investigate her symptoms?

18

It was January of 1961, a bitter cold day, but the future of our country held great promise. On January 20, John F. Kennedy had been inaugurated as the thirty-fifth president of the United States.

I was just like a lot of other teenage girls, all wrapped up in myself. I was as bubbly as soda pop. Oscar Wilde once said: "Popularity is important, without it people may not like you."

I got lonesome when Mike went away. I was crazy about a young James Dean look-alike who had sparkling blue eyes and a black Ford coupe. One summer, I had a romance with Billy Knight, a handsome, sandy-haired lifeguard with muscular legs and soft brown eyes. To many a teenage girl, these attributes were the criteria for romance. Since Mike threatened the lives of many of my boyfriends, the ranks began to dwindle.

In time, princesses and popularity fade. My days as a golden girl would soon end abruptly. There were undercurrents of unrest within my family. I was working in my father's store after school and on Friday nights, but the candy store had lost its glamour for me. This was my father's life, not mine. I wanted to be free, to find my own place in life. My parents weren't interested in my schoolwork or education. I bought into the promises of being popular and having boyfriends. I regret that I didn't pay more attention to my own future.

I wanted to go away to college and was surprised when I was accepted at the University of Bridgeport, Connecticut. I was drifting away from my family and their emphasis on materialism. My home environment seemed distant and superficial. I had a feeling that something was wrong, a force that threatened all of us. It was almost as if an evil presence was about to invade our perfect world.

It was my senior year in high school. My mother's face had grown thin and strained. She didn't smile like she used to. Instead, her bow-shaped lips grew taut, she looked troubled. Mother had lost a lot of weight, and it showed in her face. Her skin was stretched too tightly across her cheeks, giving her a sunken appearance. Her blue eyes took on a dull, grayish tint. Something was amiss.

I realize that there were too many demands on my mother. I'm glad I'm not beautiful, leaving me with too many dreams to fulfill, and too much to lose. The passing years can be unkind to a woman who was once the center of attention. She became disillusioned with the life she had worked so hard to create.

Mother was always very modest—she always wore tailored, conservative clothes—but she had taken to wearing loose, unflattering attire. The effect was perplexing. I wondered why Mother had suddenly become suspicious of me, my friends, and my boyfriends.

Dad, instead of praising her, grew more and more critical, constantly questioning her behavior. Was my mother just a younger, trophy wife? What was happening?

My Mother had a wonderful, trusted friend named Lorraine. Lorraine and her husband tried to help, but at the time, their advice made my mother more agitated. Still, Lorraine was a good friend, to the end.

Senior year in high school was one of unrest. I was uncomfortable with rumors of my mother's odd behavior. Not only was my popularity waning, I also had chicken pox and missed two weeks of school. My face was red, itchy, and pockmarked—Mike feared I would have scars for life. I was forbidden to go in the sunlight, forcing me to stay in my darkened room. My spirits were very low. My grades were suffering, and I barely passed my history exam.

Graduation night at Asbury Park High School was a time of parting from old friends and my old life. Miraculously, my face had healed from the lesions. I walked down the aisle with Eddie Golden, whom I always liked and was one of my earliest crushes. Convention Hall was crowded with relatives and friends of the graduates. I wore my favorite emerald green sheath and dyed-to-match shoes. My blonde hair was done in a soft pageboy, and I was full of youthful expectancy. I couldn't eat dinner that night—my stomach was churning. I was apprehensive about my future. One of the boys gave me a swig of vodka, which stung my insides like a scorpion.

A milestone in my life. I had graduated high school, but where was I to go next? I was accepted at the University of

Bridgeport, but my parents were having problems. Within a few months, my mother had a nervous breakdown. In July, my father told me: "You can't go away to college. Your mother is sick. Besides, I don't have the money to send you away to college."

"You don't have the money? You're a successful businessman. You own two stores!"

He dropped his arms to his side, tilted his head, and looked me in the eye. "What does a woman need college for? It's a waste of money. Go back to high school for graduate studies."

"What? I'm already accepted."

"Shush! You're not going—that's final!"

I was devastated.

My father's logic must have been the inspiration for the Taliban's insistence that women remain uneducated.

My head was spinning. I had nightmares about my future. There I was, a gray-haired matron, standing behind the candy counter, wearing squeaky white rubber-soled shoes, shifting my weight from foot to foot and waiting on customers.

"May I help you?" I heard myself saying in a grandmotherly voice. I could almost feel the soreness in my back and the painful corns on my feet. There was nowhere to sit down, not a chair in sight. The waistband on my uniform had grown tight and I was missing a button. I had eaten too many chocolates over the years.

My father was still standing over my shoulder.

"The customer's waiting. Remember, when you make up the boxes, don't smash the marshmallows."

"Yes, Dad. I know, I've been doing this since I was ten years old," I snapped.

The vision faded.

Maybe I should get married.

19

Every child has a hiding place, and my hiding place was the dusty attic that ran across the top of our house. A long flight of stairs led from the second floor to a landing on the third floor, then four more steps led to the attic itself. Hand-hewn rafters supported the roof, and the natural wood floors were rough with splinters. The attic was cool and somewhat dark, except for one naked light bulb that buzzed off and on eerily, but it was a great place to hide and read books. The rain coaxed out the smell of aged timber, and the sweet scent rose in my nostrils as incense. In the far corner was my old baby crib, standing there as if expecting a new arrival. My brothers' Lionel trains were huddled in boxes against the wall and only left the station at Christmas.

As the rain beat down on the old casement windows, I cranked them half open to let in the fresh scent of rainwater. I opened the glass doors of the painted blue bookcase and searched for my favorite book, *Heidi*. I imagined that I was Heidi, living high in the Alps, high above the valley below. From my third-floor vantage point, I could see the grandfather oaks waving their gawky arms skyward. I listened to the soothing patter of the rain and pretended that I was safe and cozy, nestled in my straw bed in Alm-Uncle's attic?

The attic was dark, but light streamed in from two graceful windows. One faced east, the other west, so the attic was always bright in the rising sun and soothing in the setting sun. On rainy days, I pulled the chain of the lone bare bulb, and passed the afternoon in solitude. I could write and draw, accompanied only by the summer rain. A curious spider might peek out from the rafters, but otherwise the attic was my private refuge. What a glorious escape to run up the stairs and hide from the demands of family life. In the corner stood my old dollhouse, its white lattice-trimmed windows looking out for the little girl who used to come to play. The metallic green bushes and red tulips still framed the front door, but the tiny, lacquered furniture had vanished, along with the wooden figurines. The dollhouse, which strangely resembled my mother's house, was empty.

The attic had actually saved my life. When I was about nine years old, a nor'easter swept through the Jersey Shore, uprooting trees and ripping up parts of the Asbury Park boardwalk. During the storm, a massive oak crashed into the roof at the front of our house only seven feet above my bed. I still remember the huge roots poking up like tentacles toward the sky. My bedroom was located on the second floor; if it hadn't been for those sturdy attic rafters, I would have been killed in my sleep. The good Lord spared me.

When storms came, thunder shook the rafters and the beams groaned and trembled in the wind. The house became a tall ship, riding out the storm like a gale on the high seas. Lightning threatened the hundred-year-old oaks, flashing against the panes of the chipped casement windows. Each strike was mirrored in my eyes, but I withstood the storm. I was only a child, and little did I know that I would have many more storms to weather.

Later, at seventeen, I retreated to the attic, sneaking up the three flights of stairs and hiding from the specter of mental illness. When the rain came, I reassured myself that somewhere the rain was falling on a happy home.

Some days, squirrels and raccoons made the attic their home, and the only sound was the scratching of their nails on the rough floor, along with the sound of the rain echoing through the rafters. But I would be gone.

Leo Tolstoy once said: "All happy families are alike; each unhappy family is different in its own way." I often wondered if our family would ever be happy again.

Visions of old movies haunted me. Those old movies seemed much more sinister in black and white. I had flashbacks of Jane Eyre, and the frightening discovery that was revealed on her wedding day. The thoughts raced through my head. I began to fear the responsibilities of marriage and motherhood; maybe I would go crazy too. Maybe I *was* crazy!

My mother was getting worse. She was spending wildly, buying clothes and luxuries she didn't need. She frowned a lot, and her soft features grew strained. My father took her to a doctor after she complained of "heart palpitations" and fatigue, then he took Mother to another psychiatrist who prescribed medication to calm her down. It had the opposite effect.

Was this behavior the change of life, or just the beginning of a nervous breakdown? My mother had seemed to lose her enthusiasm, her zest for life. Going to the beach was stressful and even her white bathing suit took on a gray tinge.

I was seventeen now, having just graduated high school, old enough to be disquieted by womanly concerns. Sexual discussions between mother and daughter were discouraged, but I recognized her lack of interest in life. I wondered where my mother's passion had gone. She shunned her glamorous gowns and active social life. Her once soft features appeared strained and frown lines were beginning to appear at the corners of her mouth. This disconcerted me. Here I was, struggling with my own adolescence and reaching out for my own identity while my mother was losing not only her womanhood, but her mind as well.

I peeked into her bedroom closet, running my fingers against her favorite powder-blue taffeta gown, now pushed to the back of the rack. Nearby, a white peignoir set wilted like a faded lily from a twisted hook along the wall. There, slumped on the hardwood floor, sat her silver metallic pumps, blistered by the sun and peeling at the heels.

The bedroom was papered with purple and white wallpaper—a paisley print swimming with flowery scrolls, dots, and patterns. I thought it was gaudy, but my mother loved it. If you stared at the wallpaper long enough, the contortions could make you crazy. Even the wallpaper was beginning to curl at the edges.

Ironically, years later I read a fictional short story called "The Yellow Wallpaper." It was the story of a woman who kept staring at the wallpaper in her bedroom until the shapes and patterns transformed themselves into menacing configurations. The woman hid in her room and stared at the wallpaper until it seemed to come alive and take on a life of its own. Finally, the patterns took over her mind, and the woman had a total emotional breakdown. I couldn't get the story out of my mind. Somehow it reminded me of my mother and her purple paisley wallpaper.

My parents' bedroom was decorated with a maple bed, beige satin bedspread, and a mirrored dressing table. I would sit at the dressing table and brush my hair a hundred times, just as young girls were told to do.

One day, as I sat brushing my hair, I noticed a large, round hatbox peering out from under the far corner of my mother's bed. I set my hairbrush down and pushed the bedspread aside. I leaned over and tugged on the braided cord, revealing a dusty red-and-black hatbox. Carefully, I brushed off the dust and lifted the lid, exposing crinkly layers of faded tissue paper. I pushed the paper aside. Inside, cozy as a kitten, was a lovely wide-brimmed hat. I reached into the box and examined the delicate confection. The material was as fine as woven black lace, but sturdy enough to have an elegant, wide brim. The brim was adorned with a single red-silk rose. The hat was in pristine condition and could easily have adorned the cover of *Vogue* magazine. In fact, Bette Davis wore an identical hat in the movie *Dark Victory*.

I rustled the tissue paper, then carefully lifted the hat from its crinkled shrine. I sat down in front of the mirror and cautiously placed the hat on my head. I was Scarlett O'Hara, primping before her anticipated visit to Tall Oaks and her beloved Ashley Wilkes. Hesitantly, I glanced into the mirror. Where was the self-conscious, uncertain adolescent who was casually brushing her hair a few minutes before? I was surprised to see she had disappeared.

My simple, blonde pageboy haircut framed my face, and suddenly the tomboy was gone, replaced by a slender, stylish, young woman. It seemed as if a stranger was looking back at me. I was becoming a woman. Part of me was terrified, but part of me was confident and proud. I wondered why my mother didn't wear the elegant hat anymore. It just sat in the hatbox, gathering dust. Later that afternoon, I asked my mother.

"Your father didn't like it."

Why didn't my mother wear it anyway, rather than hide it? It just flopped there like a lost daydream.

Joanie, seventeen years old

20

The Jersey Shore is hypnotic. Even the deadliest hurricane and fiercest nor'easter couldn't destroy my family's love of the sea. We reveled in the wild, unpredictable environment.

My dream was to live in a house by the ocean, but until then, I would spend the summers with my grandmother in her home, which we called "Four Atlantic," its address. Bradley Beach was a town of bungalows and white-columned colonials bordered by a jetty and wild beach dune. Driftwood often washed ashore in the nearby cove. In the fall, we could hear the autumn wind rustling like music through the tall grass.

Gran's house was full of lacquered, overstuffed furniture, but a Victorian sofa took center stage to her drab olive chairs. She was proud of her living room, but even prouder of her dining room, or "parlor." There was a side porch with a foldaway cot for visiting grandchildren. On summer nights, my grandmother and I would climb the steep "wooden hill" to the upstairs bedroom and fall asleep listening to the sea.

I can still hear the clanging of the buoy as it echoed off the Avon jetty, lulling me to sleep. One fall evening, after a fierce nor'easter, the buoy was silent. The steel sentinel had broken loose from its mooring and washed ashore on the Avon beach. The next morning, Gran and I walked down to the beach. We mourned as we spied the buoy run aground in the windswept sand. Little white gulls circled the fallen red framework as the buoy lay forlornly on its side. The bell was hushed, and the inlet was defenseless.

How I miss the lonely sound of the buoy as it rang across the sea. In the early 1950s, Gran and I spent our summers swimming, gathering shells, and reading. Unless there were fresh puddles to splash in, rainy days were the best days for reading. My favorite books were *Heidi*, the *Wizard of OZ*, and *Alice in Wonderland*. I identified with Heidi, who lived an idyllic existence in the mountains with her grandfather. All I needed was a couple of cows to call home. The end of summer was a sad time for me. I would gather up my shells and memories, then wait for my father to bring me home. Summer was over.

Gran was fiercely independent, and a teetotaler. Gran always said: "Lips that touch wine will never touch mine." She didn't smile much, but she possessed a great wit. Together we guarded a vague premonition of the gathering storm—my mother's madness lurked in the shadows like a hobgoblin. We feared that a stranger was waiting beneath those bright blue eyes. Mother seemed to be lost in a maze, and her mind was unraveling like a ball of twine. Unlike Theseus, she could not find her way out of the maze.

Plutarch, in his *Letter of Consolation to his Wife*, states, "If we cease to grieve, we may cease to remember."

Mother had been behaving strangely. It happened in 1962, when I was only seventeen. My grandmother and I were awakened in the middle of the night by the sound of shouting. My mother was screaming at the top of her lungs, my father being the object of her rage. This was unusual because my mother was quiet and ladylike. My parents never fought. To outsiders, our mother was the perfect wife and mother. Yet, underneath the façade, something was threatening us all.

Years later, I realized that my mother was really a warm, loving person when she married, but the demands of being a wife and mother may have transformed her into an uptight stereotype of the perfect wife. The scream in the night never happened again. Instead, it was replaced by an uneasy tension. Even my mother's once melodious laugh sounded strained. There was a nervousness in her mannerisms, and a lack of confidence uncharacteristic in a beautiful woman.

My mother became increasingly short tempered. Gran thought my mother was irritable because she wasn't eating properly and had lost more than ten pounds. Gran was a small boned, slender woman; my mother was taller and big boned. Like me, she had a tendency to gain weight around the middle. A steady diet of her homemade chiffon pie didn't help. Soon my mother became suspicious of her friends and family and began to withdraw from reality.

I knew my mother was sick before anyone else. I told my father, but he refused to listen. There were subtle changes in my mother's appearance. Her face looked thin and drawn, and her skin was dry. Even her makeup appeared harsh. The deep pink lipstick appeared garish on her soft white complexion and her pale-blue eye shadow looked caked and dried. She forbad me from borrowing or trying on her clothes, which were beginning to sag on her gaunt frame.

When my mother complained of not feeling well, the doctor diagnosed her as a hypochondriac. She appeared drawn and tired, and worse, suspicious. This was the beginning of her paranoia. A few months later, my mother turned against my father, my grandmother, and me. I had just graduated from high school. It was a tough time for me, and I was too immature to deal with the situation. My two brothers were only fourteen and nine years old. I couldn't understand what was happening to our family.

What went wrong? We were highly respected not only in the community, but also in the Greek Orthodox Church. What did my father do? Nothing! He was busy in the store. He was a hardworking, successful businessman, well respected and loved by his family, blindsided by my mother's illness, and unable to find a solution. He rationalized mother's behavior on his wife being a woman, and therefore unable to control her emotions. Besides, he thought, her behavior could be explained—his family insisted that Mother was overly emotional because she wasn't Greek. That made sense to my father. Why hadn't he thought of that himself?

Soon my family and I began to live in fear of Mother's unpredictable behavior. Clearly, something was wrong.

When my mother had a breakdown, my father's solution to the problem was threefold.

First, my father thought that if he ignored the problem, it would go away. After all, his business took precedence over everything, even family problems. This worked for a while until my mother's behavior became uncontrollable. One afternoon, I watched in horror as my mother took off her high-heeled shoe and jabbed it into my father's palm, drawing blood. There must have been some feminine imagery in this act—my mother never did like high heels.

Second, my father decided to take Mother to a psychiatrist. For months he had ignored the problem, now he *had* to do something. He was advised to take Mother to a shrink. Surely, a psychiatrist could diagnose the problem. Dad called a psychiatrist to the house; the doctor almost fell down the front steps as he was leaving. He shook his fist at my father and shouted, "Your wife needs love and attention!"

Third, since that advice didn't sit well with Dad, he took Mother to another psychiatrist, who treated her with medication. The medication caused Mother to lose all control. She became delusional and disoriented.

A visible animosity had sprung up between my parents. My mother became more and more short tempered. Her clothes hung loosely on her once shapely figure. Once, she even came downstairs flouncing about in her pink peignoir set, something she had never done before. This was totally out of character for a woman who had been the model of refinement and sophistication.

Then it happened. The scream in the night. I knew that was the end of my parent's marriage. My parents never fought, so it was unusual when we were awakened at midnight by my mother's screaming She was standing in the hall in her nightgown, screaming at my father. Her face was wildly contorted, and her lipstick took on a garish mauve tint in the lamplight. Gran and I came running out of the room.

"What's wrong with Mother?" I shouted at my father.

"Nothing! Nothing!" he scowled.

"What do you mean?" I pleaded, "she never yells like that!"

Mother kept screaming.

"It's all your fault, Angy, all your fault," she shrieked.

"I hate you for all you've done to me—everything! Everything! Do you hear me? You never listen to a thing I say. Never! I hate you!"

My father tried to quiet her, but she beat his chest with her fists. Then she fled to her room and began sobbing.

I was terrified. I had never seen my mother yell and carry on like this. My brothers stood by the doorway to their room, wondering what was happening.

"Go back to bed, all of you. I'll take care of this!" my father shouted angrily.

We slunk back to our rooms, unable to sleep. Gran just shook her head. My mother didn't even know we were there.

This outburst was an indication of trouble ahead. My mother had a total breakdown a few months later. It was one of the ugliest days of my life. It's hard for me to describe the scene, which is forever burned in my memory. I saw what happens when a man falls out of love with a woman. Now that her beauty and mind were fading, my mother was a disposable commodity.

What was marriage all about, I wondered.

Is this what being a woman comes down to? Did all the cooking, cleaning, and childbearing, the striving to be attractive and pleasing to a man, come to this abrupt end? I learned that being a woman in my family didn't count for much. My mother was discarded like a bundle of old clothes.

As Ralph Ellison wrote in *Invisible Man*:

> Why do I write, torturing myself to put it down? Because in spite of myself I've learned some things. Without the possibility of action, all knowledge comes to one labeled 'file and forget,' and I can neither file nor forget.

I'll never forget the day the paramedics drove up to my house, the day that I realized there was injustice in the world. It was the time when I was young, pretty, and popular. It was the time before the flashbacks, the flashbacks of an eighteen-year-old girl standing in her elegant living room, watching as the ambulance attendants administered a knockout sedative to her beautiful mother. This scene was forever reflected not only in the prisms of mother's prized crystal chandelier, but also in my mind.

Two white-coated men had emerged from an ambulance, walked up the stairs, and barged into our home like terrorists. The door slammed shut behind them. My father seemed to be directing this operetta, as he led them into the living room. Quickly they surrounded my mother and talked quietly to her. They assured her that she was going to the hospital, where she would receive help.

"No! No!" she shouted, "I'm not leaving my home! This is my home, get out! Get out!" She flashed her blue eyes at my father and frowned.

"You did this to me, didn't you, Angy?" she sobbed. He stood silent.

She pulled away from them. They grabbed her, pushed her down on the sofa and gave her an injection in her arm. She became woozy and almost passed out. As I stood by and watched the paramedics administer the knockout shot, I felt the needle pierce my soul. I felt my mother's pain and anguish. Her very own husband, the man who had once loved her, the man who married her and taken her out of a life of poverty, had betrayed her. Now she was tossed aside like a battered kewpie doll. Her blue eyes fluttered and began to droop, as her carefully waved blonde hair fell softly on the deep purple sofa.

As she passed out, my body felt as if it was floating across the room, while I was frozen to the floor. The paramedics lifted her slender body onto a gurney and whisked her out the door. I can still hear the clack, clack, clack of the stretcher clattering down the front steps like a runaway train.

I was seventeen. The mother I had known was gone. My mother was wheeled into the ambulance and whisked away to an unknown fate. I relived this scene years later, as I watched my son and husband, as they, too, were carried away in ambulances, accident, and stroke victims.

This part is almost impossible to write, it's too painful, but it's a story that I must tell, directly and honestly. I was standing apart from the scenario as my spirit temporarily left my body, while some other girl stood in my place. Her iron-shod feet fixed her to the floor. I felt as if I had a stand-in, a double. It was a nightmarish experience.

Now my mother became the victim of an incompetent and insensitive mental health care system. It was a nightmare come to life, a beautiful woman in a madhouse. No one should ever have to watch his or her parent being "put away."

I write these words to bare my soul. I'm tired of hiding the pain and putting on a brave face for the world. I'm tired of lying about the truth and creating a façade of fantasy. I hope my words will give others strength, compassion, and understanding toward their loved ones. I want to tell others that in my mother's case, there *was* hope in dealing with mental illness.

My father went to visit my mother in Marlboro Hospital. He became a broken man, sad, but resigned to the fact that he had "put her away." His life, too, fell apart. Here was our father, a man we loved and respected, a successful businessman and family man, reduced to a villain. I guess he thought that hospitalization would solve the problem, but at the time mental health care was still in the dark ages, still taboo. Women's health problems were viewed as "all in their mind" or "looking for attention."

The clinical diagnosis was paranoid schizophrenia. She was admitted to a "cottage" with other women, where she would receive treatment. This was the beginning of her descent into the abyss. The prognosis wasn't good. The doctors administered shock treatment without her consent. Many of her memories were wiped out forever.

Three weeks later, my well-meaning Uncle Ken drove to the hospital, signed her out, and brought her home. Her life was shattered. She wasn't the same. Neither were we. Maybe we could have done more. Maybe we panicked. Did my father think he was helping his wife, or did he just want to be rid of her? I'll never know. I have learned to forgive my parents for their mistakes. I hope my children will forgive me for mine.

What happened to that smiling, golden-haired young woman who held me in her arms when I was a baby? It was as though a shadowy spirit had taken over our lives, suddenly there was a predator in our midst. The foreboding in my young girl's mind was swooping down on raptor's wings. My personal nightmare had taken on breath. Our family was destroyed and nothing in my life would ever be the same again. A year later, my mother threw my father out of the house. My brothers and I were left alone. Our father just concentrated on his store. The irony of it all was that we were in the candy business.

When I think of it, don't we all try to escape the trials of life?

I was heartbroken. Don't get me wrong, my father was a wonderful, charismatic man, I loved him dearly, and I was always closer to him. Now I had lost both parents. It's unfortunate that Mother eventually lost control of her life. Then again, maybe many women share the same fate. I can see where I lost control of my own life.

This is what mental illness does to a family. None of us knew what to do. We were helpless. The medical profession failed us. No one thought to counsel us as a family. We just fell apart. People saw mental illness as a stigma, and as a daughter, the stigma was passed on to me. The older I get, the more I sympathize with my mother. I realize now that motherhood is a lot more difficult and demanding than I ever could have imagined. Only when I married and had children of my own did I realize how difficult it was to be a wife and a mother. Besides, there's no retirement.

Mother came home a broken woman, even worse than before. Her eyes were like the eyes of a wild mountain lion cornered by her captors. Sometimes she stared into space, as if preoccupied. The shock treatment had changed my mother. She was such a wonderful cook, but she couldn't remember her recipes anymore. Even worse, Mother grew hostile to her own family. She struck out at me and grew angry toward my father. There was no making up. Instead of helping her, my father led her deeper into the abyss of madness. I heard him mutter the words "divorce" and "call my lawyer" under his breath. He was looking for a way out. None of us knew what to do.

Now Mother lived in a labyrinth of paranoia. The more she tried to escape, the more she became lost in the maze. Within six months, my mother threw my father out. Three months later, she told me to leave. I was eighteen. The old neighborhood would be gone forever. I guess I never got over leaving my childhood home.

I stood on the front porch, dumbfounded, looking down at my belongings. My mother had tossed my clothes into a cardboard box by the front door.

"You have to leave now!" she declared. "You can't stay here anymore."

She angrily slammed the door shut. I could hear the click of the lock, sealing my fate. I was gone, never to really live in my home again. Maybe I visited for a few months, but I never really lived there. All my memories would go with me.

The memory of that day will forever be emblazoned in my mind. The sun had reached its zenith in the sky. Even though the sun's flames were swirling furiously in the Indian summer heat, it seemed to be spiraling out of control. My world was exploding in a flash. I too, was falling. Like Icarus, I had flown too close to the sun. I plummeted toward earth. The majestic oaks nodded their heads goodbye, as the clinging breeze gathered satiny vapor from the misty lake. The empty street stretched before me. I gathered my box of clothes and headed for my car. The hot pavement burned the soles of my shoes.

I would have quoted scripture and shook the dust from my sandals, but I was an agnostic at the time. Instead, I just stood on the front steps, staring at my box of belongings. I took one long look at the empty street, the lake, and the gnarled oaks. Here I was—eighteen years old, all alone, with no money and nowhere to go.

I had no real job and wasn't trained to do anything except wait on customers in the candy store. I had the old blue '54 Plymouth that I had bought for $150. I threw my belongings in the back seat and drove away, leaving a trail of dust behind me. I lost everything that day—my home, my family, and my identity. I began to identify with the dispossessed, and to this day, I fear being homeless.

The neighborhood where I once played would be only a memory. I wondered where God was, and why He had turned his back on me. I remembered the icons in the Orthodox Church staring down at me from the iconostasis, and I vowed to stop going to church. My mother was sick, my father had left, and I had nowhere to live. All I could think of was Gran's insightful Biblical quote: "A house divided against itself cannot stand."

When I think of my loved ones today, I believe that no matter how painful love can be, it has given me a direction and purpose. And that someday I will be reunited with them in a peaceful, perfect world where pain and suffering do not exist.

There was nothing I could do but turn to Mike, my off-again, on-again boyfriend. Images of my flawed knight in shining armor, galloping to rescue his delicate princess from her stifling, vine-covered castle, drifted through my mind. There was a fairy tale quality to the whole situation, but instead of riding a white horse, my hero drove a 1960 black Ford Fairlane convertible.

I was so confused. Maybe in our human psyche, we need to invent heroes such as Ulysses and Prince Charming. My family life as I knew it was over. I was on my own.

I remembered an old book that I had read when I was a little girl. My grandmother had one of the original copies of Lewis Carroll's *The Adventures of Alice in Wonderland.* The book had both entertained and frightened me. It was a strange book, full of pen and ink drawings of Alice, the White Rabbit, the Mad Hatter, the Dormouse, and the Red Queen. The Red Queen terrified me—she was always scowling and yelling commands. I thought of the White Rabbit crying, "I'm late, I'm late for a very important date," while looking at his watch. What *was* so important about his date anyway? Funny how many of us think everything we do is so important, when in fact, most of it is meaningless.

Now I had become Alice in Wonderland. I had fallen down a rabbit hole, peered through keyholes and mirrors and was running from the Red Queen. I was running, always running—in a hurry to get nowhere. Behind me, I could hear the Red Queen shouting, "Off with her head! Off with her head!" Out of curiosity, I had followed the white rabbit, thinking him important, until I had become caught up in his fantasy. I grew taller; I shrank. I thought I would never grow old. My past was fading like the Cheshire cat—all that was left was the memory of better times, grinning in the darkness. Visions of Alice framed by golden curls and wreathed in a white dress floated before me. I was like Alice, a young girl caught up in other people's dramas.

Although Alice was the quintessential little girl who never grew up, I knew that I would face an uncertain adulthood. Someday I would have to grow up, and soon! On those front steps, I stood on the steps to adulthood. I was homeless from that day on. I identified with the less fortunate. I stopped worrying about my clothes, my appearance, and my popularity. I felt as though I had survived a shipwreck. Here I was, clawing my way up the beach, looking for a rock to cling to. It seemed as if I would run from one tragedy to another.

I felt shunned and ugly. Oddly enough, I was reading Franz Kafka's *Metamorphosis*, and identified with Gregor, the young man who woke up to find that overnight, he had been turned into a giant cockroach. This was unfortunate, but it did make him stand out in public. Fine dining would have been a problem.

I began to wonder if people were staring at me and studying my appearance, looking for the telltale signs. I already had spindly legs and brown eyes. Maybe it was happening. I touched my eyebrows for the stubble of fluttering antennae.

I had graduated high school only six months before. Now that I was homeless and transformed into a giant roach, I turned to my dark hero for consolation. In an unusual twist of fate, soon after my mother became sick, Mike's mother, Ruth, also had a breakdown. Ruth's breakdown had been brought on by a physical illness, and she, too, was hospitalized in Marlboro State Hospital. Ruth claimed she heard voices and saw mysterious symbols and writing on the wall. She was peaceful and cooperative, and the hospital released her quickly, whereas my mother had been uncooperative and angry. Since my mother didn't sign herself into the hospital, this was understandable.

21

One of my favorite books was Charlotte Bronte's *Jane Eyre*. Visions of Jane Eyre haunted me. I thought of the movie starring Orson Welles as Rochester and the gritty scene when he revealed that the woman, hidden away in the tower, was his real wife. Rochester could never marry Jane: he was married to the madwoman in the attic. The husband must lock the crazed wife away, away from friends, relatives, and society. No one must know the truth. Mental illness must be hushed up behind closed doors.

What is madness? Even today, mental illness is swept under the rug or treated with psychotropic drugs. People still turn their backs on mental illness. I cringe when I imagine my mother banished to the dark recesses of the attic and hidden in the house forever. Today, patients have the advantage of modern medicine and drugs to ease their delusions and symptoms. They didn't work for my mother and made her worse, but the drugs help some patients face the debilitating effects of mental illness. Mental illness not only threatens the patient's sanity, but the sanity of the entire family.

I wonder if some forms of madness are a sign of genius. The great composer Robert Schumann suffered from depression and died in an institution when he was only forty-five years old. His wife Clara, a concert pianist, who must have been devastated, was forbidden to visit him toward the end.

In her novel, *The Bell Jar*, Sylvia Plath describes the emotional breakdown that sadly would lead to her own suicide. Vincent Van Gogh's determination to visualize the world through his eyes may have led to his madness. If only he could have imagined the value of his paintings today.

King Ludwig of Bavaria lived to realize his dreams but bankrupted his country in the process. Today, Ludwig's castles are the highlight of a trip to Bavaria. How do you describe a genius who designed a contraption that conveyed his entire dinner table upstairs through the floor?

Is madness on the rise today? It seems that every day we read horror stories of individuals who have gone mad. Often these people are like you and me. What is it that drives them over the brink? I wonder if madness stems from the demands of society or is just a monster that lurks beneath our psyche.

Madness frightens me. It can strike anyone, at any time. Modern psychosis medicine is merely a band-aid, not a cure. Mental illness is like a rattlesnake slithering through the woods—it lies silently, but if disturbed, it coils and strikes, flinging itself against the helpless victim. It's easy to step on a rattlesnake if you're not careful. Rattlers blend in with the scenery.

How can we define madness? Is madness psychosis, lunacy, or insanity? Maybe we all have a little madness in us. Who *is* sane? Some of us express madness; others keep it just below the surface. Some of us have no problems at all.

Sometimes people with psychiatric problems hear voices, but what if the voices are real?

What if I hear voices someday? How will I know they're not real? People say that, if you're crazy, you don't know it. Maybe *I'm* crazy and I don't know it! Do you ever feel that way yourself? Maybe your friends are all nuts and *you* are the sane one? "Nope, nothing wrong with me, it's my friends who are nuts."

Maybe there's a little madness in all of us.

Gran once told me an old Pennsylvania Dutch saying: "Everyone is a little crazy except thee and me, and sometimes I'm not so sure about thee."

My mother's condition deteriorated. It was August 5, 1962. I remember standing by the kitchen table reading the headlines of the *Daily News*. Marilyn Monroe, the ephemeral film goddess, was dead. The blonde bombshell charmed and seduced a generation, having created a persona of light and fantasy.

Marilyn was Cinderella come to life, but some women's attempts to please other people often end in disaster. They become immersed in their own creation and lose their own identity.

After my mother's breakdown, people tended to see me in a different light. I had the feeling of being shunned and viewed suspiciously. What was cute or funny before suddenly became the source of whispered criticism. My appearance began to suffer, and I lost interest in clothes and socializing. I felt isolated and alone. My face broke out in chicken pox. I wasn't as important as I thought I had been.

Nothing would ever be the same again.

I wondered why no one could help us. Our family didn't deserve this! We were honest, hardworking people who were well respected in the community. Nobody in our family suffered from mental illness; where did it come from? I remember my mother complaining of "heart palpitations" and fatigue. The doctors told her it was "all in your mind."

I asked myself: "Why did God let this happen to our family?" It was so unfair, so unfair. It was a shame that our mother had to suffer, but it was an even greater shame that our family, too, had to suffer. I continue to be angry, but not at God. I am angry at the ignorance of the medical community to offer a solution. People fear mental illness as though it were contagious. Where was the counseling and understanding? Lacking such assistance, my family went our own angry ways.

Doctors didn't pay much attention to women's ailments in the 1950s and '60s. Many ailments were attributed to a woman's imagination. Five years later, when I was twenty-three, I went to a gynecologist because I thought I was pregnant with my second child. The doctor told me, "It's all in your mind."

"Joanie," he concluded, "your mother is sick, and you're only imagining that you're pregnant."

"Well, what about my morning sickness?"

"It's all imaginary," he said with a solemn face.

When I returned for a second visit three weeks later, a very red-faced doctor greeted me apologetically. I had been pregnant all the time.

22

In 1962, four months after my mother returned from the psychiatric hospital, she tossed my father's shirts, pants, shoes, suits, and ties into a suitcase and told him to leave. He never returned.

After my father left, the music in our house was silenced. One of my father's prized possessions was his upright record cabinet. Songs such as "Bloody Mary" and "I'm Gonna' Wash that Man Right Outta' My Hair" once filled the house.

The Mills Brothers' "I'll Never Smile Again" languished in the cabinet, collecting dust, and my father's favorite record, "Bell Bottom Trousers," was silenced forever.

My father's brother Tommy was a singer and musician. Tommy was the youngest of the eight brothers, and the most talented. He played the piano, clarinet, and saxophone.

It was the summer of my eighteenth birthday, and I was staying with Gran. Suddenly, we heard a knock at the door. Gran rose slowly from her chair and peered out the window.

"I think it's your father's brother," she whispered, giving me a quizzical look.

She hesitated for a moment, then opened the door.

"Hi, Aimee, remember me? I'm Angy's brother, Tommy. It's a pleasure to see you again," he said, nodding politely.

Tommy had the dark curly hair and good looks of a movie star. Gran crossed her arms and motioned him toward one of her overstuffed chairs. My grandmother didn't take kindly to my father's family, never having forgiven them for giving her daughter the thumbs down. One thing about Gran—even in poverty, she radiated class and breeding. Gran made no secret of the fact that she thought the Greeks were inferior to *her* family—the Main Line Millers of Philadelphia.

Uncle Tommy explained that he was in town this summer to do some shows at the Jersey Shore. Tommy often sang and played the music in the area. He referred to his performances as "gigs."

"Aimee, I have a gig tonight in Lakewood. I'm singing at the Laurel in the Pines Hotel. I thought I'd drop in and say 'Hi'."

At the mention of music, Gran's icy demeanor seemed to thaw. Gran was a trained pianist, and her prized possession was her old upright piano that sat, like a lost soul, in the corner of the living room. Rumpled sheet music sat forlornly above the keys, as the thumbed yellow pages curled up in memories. Her slender fingers were gnarled with arthritis, and the piano hadn't been tuned in years, but Gran could still bring tunes such as "You Are My Sunshine" and "Suwannee River" to life.

When Gran played Debussy's "Claire de Lune," her faded blue eyes would get a faraway look. She may have been lost in the past, remembering when she was young—living with her family in an elegant home with three floors of antiques. Now she was an old woman, a widow abandoned by her husband

and parents, a mother uneasy with her daughter's unraveling mind.

Gran was temporarily distracted and charmed by this suave musician sitting comfortably in the living room.

"Would you like some coffee?" Gran offered.

"Why, yes, Aimee."

Gran hustled into the kitchen and made her favorite A&P coffee while Tommy told me about his latest gig.

My grandmother soon appeared with two cups of steaming coffee and homemade raisin bread. She was beginning to let her hair down after all, which didn't happen often. Uncle Tommy and I talked about my mother and father, and how my mother was acting irrationally.

Sometimes, I think Tommy was the smartest and most charismatic man in the family, next to my father. He realized he had said enough, and tactfully changed the subject. He quietly finished sipping his coffee, turned to my grandmother, and motioned to the piano in the corner.

"Aimee, I see you have a piano. Would you like to hear me play?"

My grandmother stiffened her back against the sofa and stared straight ahead.

"Yes. There's some old sheet music on the piano."

Uncle Tommy quietly rose from the overstuffed chair and walked over to the piano. He flipped through the pages of sheet music and began to play.

His melodious voice transformed the drab room into a stage. Stephen Foster's song came to life:

I dream of Jeannie with the light brown hair,
borne like a zephyr in the summer air. . ..

My grandmother folded her arms on her lap. That faraway look glazed her faded blue eyes. If only I knew what she was thinking. I wish she had shared more of her memories with me. My shallow 1960s mind could never comprehend beyond my present situation. I wish I had developed a better understanding of her past. I could only vaguely imagine her world, a world of Victorian elegance—horses and carriages, darkened parlors, and sentimental ballads.

Everyone loved Uncle Tommy. He was a born entertainer, and he enjoyed making people happy. Even on the untuned piano, "Suwannee River" and "You Are My Sunshine" came alive.

Gran was actually staring into space and smiling. Finally, Tommy rose from the bench and announced, "Well, I guess I'd better be going. Gotta' get some rest."

"Yes," Gran perked up. "Where is the show?"

"Laurel in the Pines; it's a big old hotel in Lakewood. You have to come and see me play sometime. I sing, play the sax and clarinet."

"Thank you for visiting us," Gran nodded.

"It's my pleasure."

Uncle Tommy stood up, and with a bow worthy of Rudolf Valentino, took my grandmother's hand in his and lightly kissed her arthritic fingers.

"Goodbye, Aimee. I see you have a real appreciation of music. I'll stop by again sometime."

My grandmother rose up from her chair like the Queen of England and followed him to the door.

"Thank you for visiting," she said, locking his gaze with hers.

Then he turned toward me.

"Goodbye, Doll," he smiled, pinching my cheek.

His feet barely touched the porch as he walked down the circular steps, and into his car.

Gran stood there transfixed. "What a nice man. So talented—and to *think* that he's your father's brother!"

She shook her head in disbelief and closed the door.

23

My father called the Jersey Shore his home, and the local church was the center of his community. The parishioners were hard working and dedicated to their church and community. Father Coutros was our pastor and his wife, Presbytera, and their daughters, Helen and Kelly, were our church family.

Saint George Greek Orthodox Church had a mystical, almost hypnotic quality. Rising out of the corner of Sewall Avenue, the church was the center of worship and the stronghold of the Greek community. As a young girl, I trudged up the steep front steps and followed my parents into the narthex of the church. Slender candles flickered in the cool sand, while a silver tray awaited donations. I remember standing on tippy-toes, trying to reverence the icons.

My eyes grew wide as I kissed the gilt-framed icon of Saint George, the dragon slayer. The fierce image of the saint, the white horse, and the bloodied dragon terrified me. The dripping candles sputtered and burned behind me as acrid puffs of melting wax rose in wisps and disappeared into the shadows.

The icon of Saint George was not as impressive as the somber icon beside it. The icon of Christ looked right into my soul.

I asked myself, "Who was this Christ?"

What were these rituals all about? I believed in God, but what of this frightening story of crucifixion, death, and resurrection? There were so many questions running through my mind. My father seemed so sure of his faith; he never questioned the ancient rituals, and stood proudly through the long Sunday service, making sure we crossed ourselves and kneeled appropriately. Most of the service was in Greek. Since I didn't speak Greek, I didn't know what was happening.

I always wondered why people cried in church on Good Friday. Now I know. It wasn't just the Passion of Christ that made them cry, it's the memories of Easter celebrations with loved ones long gone. On Pascha, or Eastern Orthodox Easter, the parishioners formed a procession around the church with lighted candles. When they returned, the church doors were reopened, revealing an empty "tomb." The church was hushed in silence. Clouds of incense filled the air, clinging to our nostrils.

Father Coutros would swing the censer back and forth, bowing toward the altar. Marble pillars held the vaulted ceiling in place, while wrought-iron lamps hung ominously from the ceiling. The icons shone with shades of gold, turquoise, and crimson. Paintings of the twelve apostles circled the ceiling. A deep-red carpet rolled up the center aisle and framed the altar. The priest exclaimed, "*Christos Anesti* (Christ is risen)!" Parishioners replied, "*Alithos Anesti* (Indeed, He is risen)."

When the Royal Doors were opened, I could glimpse a miniature replica of a temple. I remember the warm, sweet wine of communion.

I always felt so ladylike in church. Most of the women wore hats or scarves, while many Yia-Yias wore black for mourning. Black was becoming to most Greek women; it set off their dark hair and high cheekbones, making them look sleek and tailored. Greek women traditionally wore black for seven years after a family member died. I would steal a glance at the older ladies' knotted hands as they crossed themselves in sadness.

My mother rarely wore black. She favored pinks, pastels, and periwinkle-blue eye shadow. Needless to say, she stood out in a sea of conservatism.

In those days, my mother was healthy, and we were well-respected members of the community.

After church, our family drove down to the boardwalk. Most of the stores in town were closed on Sundays, but the boardwalk was bustling with activity. Vendors touted hotdogs and sausage and peppers. The spicy smell of fennel, rosemary, and garlic permeated the air. Many of the vendors were Greeks, and friends of my father.

"*Tikanis*, Angy" they would shout, or "*Kali mera, koukla mou*" to me. I would shuffle my feet absentmindedly, stare at my black patent-leather shoes, and look away.

The Asbury Park boardwalk featured arcades and games of skill. "Step right up folks: pick a number and win a prize!" the barkers shouted. We put a nickel on a name or number, then watched intently as the wheel spun furiously.

"Where she stops, nobody knows," called the operator as the "click, click, click" of the wheel slowed down.

It was magical. Life is like a wheel of fortune; we never know where the wheel will land.

The subtle sleaziness of this carnival atmosphere appealed to my curiosity. It was pure honky-tonk. For a quarter, you could ride the plunging horses, mystical animals, and sea serpents, and whirl to the *oom-pa-pa* music of the pipe organ, or, as my grandmother called it, a "hurdy-gurdy." As the cymbals clashed and the drum boomed, each note attacked your senses, and the silence left you waiting for another note.

Next to Asbury Park was its opposite, the little town Ocean Grove, whose Great Auditorium was host to Methodist orators, hell-fire preachers, and choir jamborees. Billy Graham held a revival in Ocean Grove. The Methodist Camp Meeting Association founded Ocean Grove after the Civil War. On summer nights, the lyrics of the "Battle Hymn of the Republic" and "Onward Christian Soldiers" echoed through the rafters of the Great Auditorium. Sometimes on Sunday, the choir would sing the Civil War song, "Tenting Tonight": "Tenting tonight, tenting tonight, tenting on the old campground. . . ."

My mother's family summered in Ocean Grove, a favorite resort for the people of Philadelphia. Hotels such as the Quaker Inn, the Mayflower, and the Sampler Inn welcomed vacationers seeking solitude. The ocean beckoned beachgoers, but the town was strictly off-limits for revelry. Blue laws closed the town gates from midnight Saturday to midnight Sunday.

My mother's family was a mystery. My great-grandparents spent their summers in Ocean Grove, but I knew little about them. I never saw a picture of them.

My grandfather's family owned the Grand Atlantic, an elegant hotel that boasted a sweeping veranda decorated with scarlet geraniums and white rocking chairs. My grandfather was a builder who owned a series of garages for horses and carriages. He lost the garages years ago. I always suspected something, but when I asked about my grandfather, I was told that he died of a heart attack. I didn't learn the truth until I was nineteen. When I did learn the truth, I was furious! Why was the truth hidden from me?

What drove my grandfather away? I questioned everything my mother's family ever told me. Did my grandfather suffer from the same illness as my mother? How could they lie to me? How dare they deceive me by keeping the truth from me! I could never trust them again. I vowed, that if I ever had children, I would tell them the truth about their family history. How naïve I was, as one day I, too, would hide a vital truth from my children. Lying to a child is inexcusable. Although I rationalized my cowardice, my *own* future silence on a critical circumstance was *inexcusable*.

My mother's family history was cloaked in mystery. They were a family of secrets. My grandmother told us that we were related to Queen Elizabeth I of England and Queen Victoria.

It annoyed me that my grandmother's family didn't keep records of the family history or photos. If only my mother's ancestors had passed their stories down to the following generations. At least the Greeks had a history.

However, I never knew much about Yai-Yai's family. I knew her name was Anastasia Philopoulous, and that her father and brother were priests. What presence they must have had as they entered a room! I can just imagine them gliding about the altar in their long black robes, their great gold crosses clinking against their chests. Yia-Yia had another relative who my father cleverly described as an "intellectual vagabond."

I'll never know the truth about my mother's family. Regardless, I felt close to them. They were lively, intelligent people. The Jersey Shore was their life, and the sea was their religion. If Gran had only told me the truth when I was young, I would have been more understanding.

As one grows older, the past becomes more vivid. New circumstances crowd out the old experiences, but the past has a way of creeping into our dreams. I can still picture my grandmother sitting on the beach, her deeply tanned hands clasped about her knees, her white bathing suit drenched by the sun, and her watery blue eyes gazing at the sea. I always wondered what she was thinking about.

Was she sorry she left her home, or was she dreaming of the handsome lifeguard she fell in love with? She loved him once. Perhaps she still did.

I thought it was odd that she never shared any memories of him. In fact, she rarely spoke of him at all. When I was ten years old, I discovered a picture of my grandfather that had been hidden in the back of her dresser drawer, beneath a packet of rose sachet. It was an old black and white photo of a young man in an old-fashioned black bathing suit. He was slender and wiry, of average height. He stood proudly, with his hands on his hips and his eyes looking into the camera. A shock of blonde hair fell over one eye.

I always thought it strange that my grandmother didn't display a picture of her husband in the house. Was this my elusive grandfather?

I called down the stairs for my grandmother. She slowly came up the stairs.

"Who's this?" I asked with a young girl's curiosity.

"Oh, that's your grandfather."

"Why don't you keep his picture on the dresser?"

"It would make me very sad, dear."

"He's good looking, Gran. What was he like?"

"He wasn't real tall, but he was handsome, blond, and blue-eyed. He was a powerful swimmer and had very muscular arms. His name was Wilbur. I met him when he was a lifeguard in Ocean Grove. He was a fine swimmer—he just glided through the water."

She looked away.

"What happened to him?" I asked suspiciously.

"He died of a heart attack. It was quite sudden."

"Sudden?" My eyes widened.

"Yes," she sighed.

"My hair turned white overnight."

"You must have loved him very much."

"Yes, I did," she nodded. "But why don't we put his picture away for now?"

Her eyes grew moist as she opened the drawer and slipped the photo into the dovetailed corner of the dresser drawer. I never saw the photo again.

I'll never understand why women go on loving and remembering what is obviously over. I wondered if Gran was a hopeless romantic. This attribute seems to affect the women in my immediate family. Is it good or bad? Romance is thrilling, but it can also have a destructive quality clouding both men and women's judgment. I guess we just can't help ourselves.

My grandmother married for love but love disappointed her. Gran rarely shared her emotions and I wonder what she really felt inside. She was like a gnarled tree, twisted by the wind, but reaching, undefeated, toward the sky. If she became angry, she merely rose up from her chair and left the room in a huff. There were no photos, no journals—no faded letters from old lovers tied in lavender ribbons. Gran was a woman of secrets. Her family forgot her, and her husband abandoned her. Her brothers made off with her fortune.

The ocean was her fountain of youth, and her grandchildren were her consolation. The sea gave her health, strength, and vitality. She loved me, and I'll always love her as I did when I was a little girl, running toward her with open arms, still salty from the sea.

Gran's eyes grew cloudy whenever she spoke of Philadelphia. She remembered shopping at Wanamaker's Department Store, the excitement of the Mummers Parade, and the elegance of the three-tiered mansion the Millers called home. Persian rugs, fine china, and fringed lamps graced the parlor, but my grandmother left them all behind for the lure of the Jersey Shore.

I wish I had paid more attention to my grandmother's life; instead, I childishly focused on my own life. I regret that I have lost so much of my past through my own silly self-centeredness.

Who was my grandmother, this once young Aimee Millar of hidden secrets? She was born some twenty years after the Civil War. She too, had once been a young girl with dreams of love and marriage. Her Victorian world of dark parlors, upswept hair, and hushed femininity was far removed from mine. Her dreams of romance and gentility vanished in the everyday struggle of raising four children as a single mother, a life that was frowned on in those days. The Philadelphia childhood had shaped and molded her, but her upbringing had unraveled in poverty. Gran was forced to live on Relief, a government program that supplied assistance to the poor.

I vowed that my life would never be so heartbreaking. I would never marry a lifeguard. No, my husband would be faithful and true to his family. I could never live such a shabby existence. I studied Gran's meager pantry and her moth-eaten fur coat piled up on a cot on the side porch. The Mission oak table sat empty, awaiting invisible company, while the white tureens sat empty in the antique cherry cabinet. A small grandfather clock stood in the corner. The neighbors tossed it out, but Uncle Bobby dragged it off the curb and into Gran's house.

The clock stood at the head of the parlor table like the family patriarch. Maybe it took the place of our phantom grandfather. Some of the wood was peeling off the trim, but a smiling yellow moon peeked over the clock's face. The old clock kept time once, but it had stopped at twenty to nine many years before.

A white lace tablecloth clung to the parlor table like an antique shawl. The eerie claws had been carved of dark cherry wood. Rows of dust had settled in the deep ridges. I imagined that the white-lace tablecloth camouflaged a dangerous beast. It was as if the crouching table might rise up to attack me if I let my guard down. Claw-footed furniture surrounded me. The parlor chairs, sideboard, and antique china cabinet took on grotesque proportions. Even the porcelain bathtub had claw feet. Hand-carved claws clenched the armchairs: if you gripped the arms, you could imagine yourself flapping like a raptor. I thought of eagles swooping down and grasping their prey, then carrying it back to their nest. It seemed as though the furniture would rise up and fly away at any moment, or skulk across the floor at night when no one was looking.

The curtains were always closed, and the parlor had a dark aura. It reminded me of *Great Expectations*, and Miss Havisham's living room. Was this Charles Dickens' description of Satis House come to life? I envisioned swaths of cobwebs decorating the air, as Miss Havisham descended the stairs, dragging her tattered wedding garment behind her. I wondered who would rip the curtains apart and fill the room with light. I waited, but no liberator ever came. I wondered if loneliness would be my fate too.

Gran often described women who weren't married as "old maids." Once in a while we played a card game, "Old Maid." The caricature depicted a frumpy old woman who wore dowdy clothes and looked unhappy. No one wanted to be the old maid.

Was I destined to be alone, too?

No, the shabby life wasn't for me. In my young mind, I pictured the man I would marry. He would be tall and dark, a brooding Heathcliff who roamed the wild Moors. He would be a quiet man, devoted to wife and family. I could never imagine myself in such a shabby existence, wearing other people's cast-offs and hauling discarded furniture in from the street. I shook my head at the thought of rationing food and coffee.

Then there were the mice. They crept into the kitchen at night. I cringed at the thought of them squeezing their furry bodies through the cracks in the walls. I shivered at the sight of their beady eyes and rubbery tails. Sometimes I peeked in on them at night, as they skittered across the floor. They gnawed through the kitchen drawers, scampering along the counters, nibbling on tiny crumbs of raisin bread, leaving their droppings on the linoleum. In summer, they sipped the melted water that trickled under the old icebox.

The mice were smart; they waited for the heavy footsteps of the iceman who brought their libations. In the summer, the iceman would enter our domain. No gentleman caller was he, but a man of sweat and substance. The iceman was a great burly man, with rounded biceps, and a neck as strong as a tree trunk. You could hear the "thud, thud, thud" of the iceman as the sound of his heavy boots filled the house with masculinity. He would lug a huge block of dripping ice on his back through the dining room, into the kitchen, and into the gaping maw of the open icebox.

The iceman would swing the latch open, deposit the ice, then close the door like a tomb. He would wipe the sweat from his forehead with a red-checkered handkerchief and without saying a word, hand my grandmother the bill. Gran handed him a glass of water. He didn't say much, just "Thank you." Gran searched her small stash of bills and change on the table and paid him for the delivery. He nodded, turned, and left, leaving his wet footprints behind. He left quickly, like a wild animal fleeing captivity, leaving the musky scent of men's sweat hanging in the air. Gran gave him a quarter tip.

The ice took up most of the space in the icebox. On a good day, there was milk, eggs, margarine, and sliced cheese. Sometimes there were glossy red cherries, freshly picked from Gran's cherry tree. The ice would melt after a while, and the water would drip down a narrow tube beneath the icebox. It was difficult for my grandmother to bend and empty the pan of melted water.

My life could never be so heartbreaking.

I envisioned my husband and me living on an estate with thoroughbred horses, sweeping oak trees, and ponds stocked with trout. I would have a large family, an elegant home, and oh, yes, two dogs at least. I had read the books of Albert Payson Terhune and dreamt of a large Victorian home. Maybe I would have a collie and an Irish setter. I would name him Rusty, in honor of Gran's favorite companion. I dreamed of summers by the sea. I would be a well-respected member of the community who did charity work for the less fortunate. I would surround myself with intellectual people and drive a late model car. Every night we would relax at the table for dinner and conversation.

No, the shabby life wasn't for me.

24

If Gran regretted her life, she suffered in silence. Sometimes I thought that maybe it would be better if I had never married. I didn't like to cook—my idea of a meal was a tuna-fish sandwich. I never liked housework. I loved nature and the outdoors and had a habit of bringing home sick and wounded animals and trying to save them.

If I never married, maybe I would have avoided the pitfalls. Was the idea of a happy marriage just a myth?

How could I compare my two grandmothers? Gran had been raised in wealth, but now lived in poverty. It wasn't even *genteel* poverty. She welcomed company, but carefully rationed her homemade raisin bread and A&P coffee. Gran never worried about her weight, as food was a luxury. She was small, slender, and proud of her figure, even in her eighties. She was swimming in Florida's Indian River when she was ninety.

Gran had a quote for everything. "Every tub has to stand on its own bottom" was one of her favorites. When my mother became ill, my grandmother warned that "a house divided against itself cannot stand."

I always identified more with Gran, my mother's mother. I couldn't visualize myself having nine children and washing laundry in a cauldron on the stove. I wondered what happened to Yia-Yia's father and mother. I wonder if the family history would have been more inclusive if Yia-Yia had told her side of the story.

Yia-Yia was never seen in a bathing suit; Gran was buried in one. Yia-Yia chewed raw garlic, which turned Gran off.

Can you imagine describing shoofly pie to a Greek immigrant? "Flies?" Yia-Yia might question: "Why would you bake a pie that draws flies?"

Gran didn't share Yia-Yia's affinity for sautéed octopus or Papou's fondness for roasted lamb heads.

Once, when my grandfather was in the hospital, his brother brought him a roasted lamb's head for dinner. The nurse watched in fascination as, little by little, Papou ate the cheeks and forehead.

"Well, what will you eat next, Mr. Sakelaris?" the nurse asked.

He looked around the room, raised his fork in the air, and exclaimed: "The eyes!"

The nurse rushed out of the room.

When we told Gran the story, she shook her head. Then she muttered, "something wrong with those people," and left the room.

I used to ask myself if I really was related to "those people." My observations about my father's family were confirmed after a family visit to Massachusetts when I was about seven years old. Since everyone was sitting around all day talking Greek, shaking their heads, and eating, I had nothing to do. The Sakelaris family kept a few chickens in the yard, and I made a pet of one of them. Every day for a week, I snuck away to feed one of the chickens and listen to it cluck contentedly. After a few days, the chicken became my pet. One afternoon, I went out to feed the chicken, and it had disappeared. When we sat down for dinner, I asked where my pet chicken was.

"You're eating it," my father said.

My grandmothers had one thing in common: neither of them ever drove a car. Gran grew up riding in a horse and carriage, and Yia-Yia never left the kitchen. Surprisingly, there were quite a few women who never learned to drive in the late fifties and early sixties. My mother was one of them. Oh, she drove, but she didn't know how. Even when she was well, she drove through stop signs, sped to the beach, and put on lipstick while driving. My daughter drives just like her, except she's left-handed and drives on the wrong side of the road. (She thinks she's in England.)

My father never drove over the speed limit, but he drove so slowly that he often fell asleep at the wheel. Also, he ignored flashing-red railroad lights and just drove around them. Because he owned a candy store, the police never stopped him.

When my father was young, my grandfather roused him at 4:00 AM to deliver fresh bread. Papou hitched up the horse and wagon, and off they went. As they trotted through the Greek ghetto, the horse automatically stopped at each site. My father then carried the baskets of bread up the tenement's rickety stairs, knocked on the doors, and delivered the orders.

Some customers bartered with my father, paying him with various goods, such as a dead chicken or two. I can just picture this little boy carrying the bread, chickens, octopus, lamb heads, whatever, up and down the stairs. No wonder he left home at sixteen. Dad's favorite story was how a customer tried to cheat him out of the correct price. Well, this didn't sit well with my father, and he challenged the man's honesty and won.

My father learned the value of integrity at a young age. He knew the value of a dollar. When my mother wanted a washing machine, my father exploded.

"*A washing machine*? What does a woman need a washing machine for? My mother boiled all the clothes on the stove!"

My mother snapped: "With nine children, she must have used a *big* pot."

Many years later, when I was married with two children and needed a washing machine, my father turned to me and said, "A washing machine? What does a woman need a washing machine for?"

When I was twelve, I used to ask Dad for a dollar for lunch.

"What do you need a dollar for, lunch?" he gestured, waving his hands. "You don't need lunch—bring an apple. You have plenty of food at home."

The logic continued, even when I worked in the candy store.

"Hey, Dad, I worked five days after school this week; do you think I could get paid? I want to go to the movies."

My father would stop counting the day's proceeds, raise his eyebrows, and glare at me with his dark brown eyes.

"Why should you get paid for working in the store? You live in my house and eat my food. Besides, you're a girl. You don't work as hard as the boys. You are lucky—you can eat all the candy you want."

"How much candy can I eat? One cannot live on candy alone. Besides, I want to go to the movies . . .."

"Movies! Get a boyfriend to take you to the movies!"

"You don't like my boyfriends!"

"They're not Greek!"

"Oh, never mind. I give up."

"Joanie, I just don't understand you. I hope someday you have children just like you."

Is that some kind of Greek curse?

I was accepted at the University of Bridgeport, in Connecticut. Here we go again.

"College? What does a woman need college for?" my father argued. "It's just a waste of money. You'll only get married and have babies. Women don't go to college. You can always be a waitress in a Greek restaurant. It's a good living."

"Why can't I learn to make candy?"

"Make candy? You want to learn to make candy?"

"Yes, I want to learn how to make candy."

"Women *do not* make candy," he replied, shaking his head.

"Why don't women make candy?"

He stopped slicing truffles and turned toward me, waved his hand as if he were leading an orchestra, and continued.

"When you get married, you'll give all the candy recipes to your husband, then he'll open a store and put me out of business."

"Put you out of business? That's ridiculous!" I laughed. "What kind of logic is that? All I need are some recipes."

My father walked over to the nearby shelf, reached up and pulled down a well-worn cookbook. "Here's some recipes, read them." He grinned and walked away.

I opened the cookbook, only to find that it was written entirely in Greek. "Dad, it's all in Greek! You know I don't speak Greek."

"Exactly."

When I was seventeen, I bought my own car. I hated being dependent on other people to drive me around.

"A car? What does a woman need a car for?" my father shouted, slapping his palm to his forehead. "You don't need a car! Get your boyfriends to drive you around."

"What about that Italian you hang around with?" he added. "What's his name?"

"Mike, it's Mike, Dad. I've been going with him for over a year. He isn't all Italian; his mother is Irish."

"Italian and Irish? What kind of nationality is that?" he questioned. "What's wrong with you? Italians, Jewish boys, and Irish . . .."

"Boyfriends, boyfriends," he muttered, turning away. "I have to make some cashew patties."

That was that.

25

The truth was that I did have a boyfriend, maybe one or two, maybe three, but Mike was my first real boyfriend.

Mike was ruggedly handsome, a diamond in the rough. At the time, he made me feel beautiful and important.

Suddenly, I had status. There was a big Italian community in Asbury Park, and I was accepted as "Mike's girl." Pretty soon I was introduced to lasagna, antipasto, and grandpa's homemade wine. There were Saturday nights at Mom's Kitchen or Freddie's Pizzeria. Mike proudly introduced me to his relatives, who treated me as one of the family. The Italian people really impressed me with their warmth and hospitality. I was rarely home anymore, but I don't think my family noticed. My family's life revolved around the business and the house. I was expected to marry well and just go away.

Mike, in contrast, lived fast and close to life. He always worked hard. No one gave him anything. In the spring, he caddied at Jumping Brook Golf Course with his friend Warren, and in the summer, he delivered bread for Dugan's Bakery. Mike had street smarts. His father had taught him to play cards, shoot dice, and box. Mike even fought in the Golden Gloves, but his opponent was older and stronger. He knocked Mike out with one punch. From then on, Mike stuck to street fighting.

In September 1960, Mike enlisted in the Army and went off to basic training at Fort Dix, New Jersey.

"Why are you leaving me?" I anguished, feeling abandoned.

"I want to get away. Time to think about my future. They're talkin' Kansas."

"Kansas?" I gasped. "How am I to get to Kansas to see you? What's in Kansas? Corn?"

"A guided-missile site."

"You're going to work on a guided-missile site? I never saw you start a lawnmower."

"I'll learn about more than mowers," he assured me.

"The only thing you'll learn about in Kansas is corn. Besides, I'm not exactly Dorothy from the *Wizard of Oz*."

Mike shrugged.

So, Mike went off to Kansas, and I was left to dream of spinning houses and witches whining, "I'm melting, I'm melting . . . ."

The months crept by slowly, like a slug in the sand. Mike would call me from some roadhouse in the middle of nowhere, pop a coin in the jukebox, and play love songs to me. To a teenage girl, this was the epitome of romance. My phone would ring, and I could hear the whir and click of the record as it flipped onto the turntable.

Soon the receiver would bristle with static: I'm goin' to Kansas City, Kansas City here I come. Goin' to Kansas City, Kansas City here I come. They got some crazy little women there, and I'm gonna' get me one. . . .

Well, what were those lyrics supposed to mean? Did it mean Mike was going to Kansas City? Did it mean he was hooking up with "a crazy little woman" there? Or did it just mean he was waiting for a bus?

Sometimes Mike would call and say: "I picked this song just for you, here it goes."

Click, whir, flop.

Silence.

"I'll be ho-om-e my darling, please wait for me. . .."

"Uh, oh, was he coming home? What about my other boyfriends?" I frowned, pulling my ear closer to the phone. What was I to do about Billy Knight and Albert?

"Uh, oh," I thought.

The song went on: We'll walk together hand and hand, someday our hearts will be fr-e-ee.

Tears welled up in my eyes. I was such a dumb bunny.

Soon, it was Christmas. Mike would be coming home on leave. I still wore his ring around my neck on a heavy chain.

His friend Frankie dropped him off at the curb. I straightened my button-down cardigan and quickly opened the door.

There he stood, resplendent in his olive-drab uniform—beige shirt, brass buttons, pressed khakis, and crew cut. His shoes were spit-shined, and his face shone with a ruddy glow. He was trim and athletic and full of vigorous good health. He looked mature and worldly, the very qualities that drew me to him in the first place.

"Here, I brought you a Christmas present," he said awkwardly.

"Thank you!"

"It's Shalimar. Nice perfume. You'll like it."

I held the black and white box to my nose, rustling the cellophane wrapping.

"It's lovely!"

We stood there awkwardly for a moment.

"Come in, come in!" I grabbed his hand and led him to the dining room. "We have so much to talk about!"

We talked for hours, and to this day, the smell of Shalimar perfume reminds me of broken dreams.

Soon Mike was gone again—back to Kansas. He didn't like to stay in one place too long. He had a restless spirit, and after a year, he became disillusioned with the military.

"I thought I'd be working on guided missiles," he confessed.

"What are you working on?" I asked.

"Lawnmowers."

Mike came home and enrolled in Murray State College, in Murray, Kentucky. He reunited with his old friends from Asbury Park. To Mike, a friend was a friend for life.

The 1960's were a time of social unrest and upheaval. Being a northerner, Mike wasn't accustomed to the prejudice he encountered in the South. He was surprised that many students had boycotted Jackie Wilson's performance at the college. He couldn't understand discrimination and chose to hang out with his northern friends. His year at Murray State was an awakening for him. He settled into studying history and decided he wanted to be a lawyer.

I encouraged Mike to go to college, but Mike's interest in history didn't come from me at all. Mike always credited Lucille King, his friend's mother, for encouraging him to study history. Lucille gave Mike books about Hannibal and Tamerlane and told him of her family ties to President James Monroe. In later life, Mike took a deep interest in politics and the history of World War II. He always thought it was a bad omen that he was born on December 7, 1941.

He always said, "I know I have a dark cloud that follows me. . . ."

Joanie and Mike, late 1950s

26

I keep asking myself: "Did my mother's breakdown stem from a physical illness, or did the change of life have anything to do with both Mike's mother and my mother's breakdowns?"

They were the same age, Ruth being a little older. Her mother had suffered from some illness, and Mike always thought that he, too, would inherit the disease. He was at Northern Illinois College, spending a semester washing dishes in the college cafeteria, at the time, so he didn't learn of his mother's hospitalization until he came home. Since Mike was more independent than I was, my first reaction was to drive over to Mike's house and ask for help.

The Corcione family welcomed me and offered me a place to stay, but I couldn't accept—it wouldn't have been right. Mike suggested I call my old friend Suzanne, who had been on her own since she was seventeen. I've always been blessed with good friends. I believe that God sends us angels in the form of friends—not only do they appear from nowhere, they also appear at just the right time.

Suzanne had been my friend for a couple of years. She was a little older than me, but wiser. We often met at Suzanne's house on Saturday nights. She was tall and slender, but didn't stand out in a crowd. She had pale-blue eyes and medium length natural blonde hair. Suzanne was a quiet girl, and somewhat self-conscious. She didn't compete with the other girls and had mastered self-control. She dressed conservatively and seemed more mature than other girls her age. She lived in Wanamassa, a community next to Asbury Park, in a sturdy Tudor home that conspicuously graced a small corner lot. A great stone chimney faced the side street.

One item I remember about Suzanne's house was a photograph of her father. The old photo held a place of importance on the dining-room table. Her father's handsome face rested comfortably in its warm sepia background. His eyes were gentle and brown, and the visor of his regulation Army hat barely shaded his strong forehead. The photo was Suzanne's only remembrance of her father. He had been killed in the Second World War.

The sepia made a lovely background for a photograph; it softened the features and gave the picture an air of melancholy.

The photo was a ghostly reminder of the father Suzanne never knew. I don't think Suzanne's mother got over losing her husband in the war. She lived a solitary life, but encouraged her daughter's friends to hang out at her house. It was a good strategy, and it kept us kids off the streets. Suzanne was always calm and understanding towards her mother, but one day they had a falling out and now Suzanne, too, was on her own. When I called her and told her of my plight, she suggested we get an apartment together.

As ridiculous as it sounds at the time, many landlords didn't want to rent to single women. We tried a lot of places, and, somehow, ended up in an apartment in Ocean Grove. The Ocean Grove Camp Meeting Association had fashioned small cottages around the Great Auditorium. The cottages had raised porches and cozy canvas entryways.

The town featured a pristine beachfront complete with pavilions and an extended fishing pier. The streets had unique names such as Pilgrim Pathway and Mount Herman Way. Hotels such as the Quaker Inn, and the Grand Atlantic beckoned vacationers. Colorful gingerbread houses rose up out of neatly trimmed lots. My great-grandparents were drawn to Ocean Grove by the cool summer breezes and sweet salt air.

Suzanne and I decided that Ocean Grove was the safest place for two young women. As we drove through the wrought-iron gates, I couldn't help thinking how odd it was that I was returning to my ancestral town. I wondered if my great-grandparents were looking down on me. My life had come full circle.

Since we didn't have much money, we looked for a place that was reasonable. We drove around and stopped in front of a gray Queen Anne home with a tiny porch and a window box blooming with purple ageratum and red geraniums.

The sign in the window read: "Room for Rent." We pulled up to the curb and knocked on the door. After a minute or two, a lean face peered out from between the sunlit curtains. We waited, and soon an old woman opened the door. She was tall and slender, and her gray hair was piled up around head. She wore dark stockings and a black-crepe dress that almost brushed her ankles. The woman wore no makeup, and her translucent skin was stretched tightly over her high cheekbones. She looked as if she had just stepped out of the Victorian Age.

Suzanne cleared her throat.

"Do you have a room for rent?"

"Yes, I have a room for rent. It rents by the month. I require one month's security. It's $50 a month."

Suzanne and I nodded to each other.

"May we see the room?" I asked politely.

"Why yes, come in. It's up the stairs."

We stepped into a small foyer. To our right stood a cozy parlor, complete with an ornate sofa, a rocking chair, and a dark mahogany table. Purple African violets flourished beside the white lace curtains. The room was spotless and inviting.

We held on tight to the banister as we followed her up the stairs.

She reached into her pocket and pulled out a long key.

"It's a nice room. Has a bath, too," the woman stated proudly, unlocking the door.

The bedroom was bright and airy. The hardwood floors were shiny and swept clean. An old brass bed stood in the corner, dressed in a white chenille spread and pale blue quilt. There was a small night table to the right, highlighted by a graceful Tiffany lamp. The only sound in the room was the "tick, tick, tick" of the old Seth Thomas clock on the far shelf.

"The sitting room is over there," she said, pointing to a narrow doorway.

We took a few steps and noticed a light pine desk with a pen, pink stationery, and a matching rose-patterned chair. Lovely.

"This is the bathroom," she nodded, guiding us around the corner toward an old claw-foot tub with a small tag on the spigot.

We walked back to the bedroom. The summer sun was streaming through the window, highlighting the clean, tidy rooms. The woman folded her arms in front of her, then quickly unfolded them and pointed to the bed.

"See this bed? All clean sheets. There ain't no buggers in here! I can tell you that—no buggers in here!" she insisted, shaking her head.

To this day I can't remember the old woman's name, but from then on, we always referred to her as "Mrs. Buggers."

The woman straightened her shoulders.

"No male visitors are allowed," she announced with all the authority of a Girl Scout leader. I looked at Suzanne and she looked at me.

"We'll take it," Suzanne and I nodded in unison.

We had found a safe place to live.

The next morning, we arose early to go to work. Suzanne was working as a dental assistant and was doing well. I was still working in the candy store and sometimes waited on tables at a local restaurant.

It was summer. There was something cheerful about the summer candies. The cases were filled with salt-water taffy and brightly colored bon-bons. No matter what was happening, my father made wonderful candy. He took great pride in his creations, especially the bon-bons. First, he filled a big metal pitcher with creamy white fondant, then he picked up small rounds of peanut butter, dipped them into the fondant one at a time and set each one on a crisp piece of white paper to dry. My job was to sprinkle the tops with chopped walnuts. When my father wasn't looking, I would lean over and eat a peanut butter bon-bon. I was amazed at the contrast between the rich white fondant and the velvety peanut butter.

Sometimes more than one bon-bon, possibly two or three, disappeared. I became very adept at sneaking them away from their neat rows. My father would count them and just look at me, then clean out the metal pitcher, add more fondant, and add some lemon or raspberry food coloring and make more bon-bons. Miraculously, the food coloring turned the fondant bright lemon or lavender. He also dipped a tray of coconut or raspberry rounds into the fondant.

"White cups! White cups! Always use white cups," my father insisted, reaching under the counter for the crinkly papers.

When he completed the process, he had created an assortment of white, raspberry, and lemon bon-bons, which he set on the tray to dry. My job was to put the bon-bons in cups and arrange them for display in the cases.

I enjoyed plopping the colorful bon-bons in white cups, lining them up in rows, and displaying them in the candy case. Sometimes I think my father was an artist, as the display was like a study in still life. The complimentary arrangement of white, lavender, and yellow reminded me of Van Gogh's *Irises* and the vivid flowers that grew wild outside my mother's porch.

Things were going along peacefully for the most part. Suzanne was working, I was working, and my father had his business to keep him occupied. My mother was still sick. Other than the fact she had given her bedroom set to the garbage men and bought two mink coats, everything was peaceful.

My mother's lawyer told her, "Your husband is responsible for all your bills," so Mother acted accordingly. Who could blame her? She hid the mink coats, and my father never found the furry luxuries.

I was as guilty as the rest of the family, thinking that if we ignored mental illness, it would go away. I didn't see much of my mother during those years. Nor did she make an attempt to see me, so I let it go at that. I think my mother needed solitude and healing. Later, she swore that she "felt better after Angy left."

Once in a while, she would show up at the store. Mother needed help, and she needed money to run the house. My father begrudged her demands. He would walk around the store muttering, "I hate you, Margie, I hate you, Margie" under his breath. Sometimes I thought both my parents were going crazy. Sometimes I thought *I* was going crazy! I became paranoid about trickle-down mental illness. I never really felt like a schizophrenic, but sometimes I was beside myself.

Meanwhile, Suzanne and I were relaxing in our new apartment. There were a few problems though. The second night we were there, I decided to take a nice, warm soak in the rustic, claw-footed tub. As I turned on the faucet, I noticed a small white tag attached to the handle. Bending closer, I read the writing—*Baths: .25.*

I couldn't believe my eyes. What was this, the YWCA? I pushed the tag aside and turned on the water. As the water rose a few inches in the tub, Mrs. Buggers came flying up the stairs like Norman Bates in drag.

"Do you see that sign there, young lady?" she huffed, placing her hands on her hips in defiance. "It says, '25 cents a bath.' You have to pay me twenty-five cents for each bath. I keep track of all expenses, and I run my house well!"

I turned off the faucet, grabbed a towel, and walked over to the sitting room. I took a quarter out of my purse and handed her the quarter. Mrs. Buggers looked at the quarter and closed her palm.

"And don't use too much water!" she cautioned. "You only need a foot of water to take a bath, and you don't need a bath every day!"

She held her head high, then gathered her long skirts in her hand and shuffled down the stairs. Suzanne started laughing hysterically.

Mrs. Buggers' voice rose from the bottom of the stairway. "I'll have none of that, young ladies! None of that!" She stopped to turn off the lavender globe lamp by the banister, then disappeared into the parlor.

Suzanne had buried her head in a pillow to keep from laughing. She had a wonderful laugh.

When I look back, I realize how lucky we were to be staying in such a clean, safe environment. We spent the summer there amid ocean breezes and cool summer nights. We were careful to keep our rooms clean and not bring young men into Mrs. Buggers' sanctuary. Mrs. Buggers lived in her perfectly preserved Victorian world, and although we thought her a little odd, we respected her.

Mrs. Buggers was very strict about "gentleman callers." They were only permitted as far as the front porch. Not only was our landlady protecting us, she was protecting herself as well.

We didn't know much about Mrs. Buggers' personal life. There weren't any photographs visible. She led a solitary life and closed off the outside world. She was wary of the presence of men, and years later, I came to respect her judgment. Now I realize that Mrs. Buggers was a very smart, frugal woman.

It annoyed Suzanne and me that we couldn't invite our boyfriends to our apartment. We had to meet them elsewhere or have them wait restlessly on the front porch until we came to the door. Also, due to Ocean Grove's blue laws, no traffic was allowed in Ocean Grove on Sundays. After midnight on Saturday, drivers parked their cars outside the town and walked home. Residents and visitors crossed over Wesley Lake via a small bridge that led from Asbury Park to Ocean Grove. Ocean Grove was a dry town—no liquor and no bars. This never bothered me much, because the bar scene wasn't for me. Besides, I was food oriented and too short to get up on a barstool gracefully.

Gradually, Suzanne and I decided to look for another apartment. We found a nice apartment in Asbury Park and left Mrs. Buggers forever. Now our boyfriends could visit us openly. This sounded good at the time. As I said before, the older I become, the more I admire the wisdom of Mrs. Buggers.

I was still working in the candy store and making very little money. I was beginning to enjoy living on my own and being away from my family. I was in survival mode, still seeing my father every day at the store, but my mother was a memory, and a sad one at that.

27

Around that time, my father, being lonesome and needing attention, started keeping company with a lady friend. Her name was Anita, and she owned The Little Campus, a small restaurant on Main Street in Asbury Park. Anita was a fabulous cook. A 100% Greek, she, too, had grown up in Massachusetts.

Anita was of Spartan and Macedonian descent, had fair skin, natural blonde hair, and lively blue eyes. Not tall, but she had a nice figure and an engaging personality. She dressed simply and modestly. Anita never wore makeup, but with her fair coloring and pale eyes, she resembled a less glamorous version of my mother. When she married her husband, Lambert, she taught herself how to cook and run a restaurant. Lambert had once coached an Asbury Park baseball team, and by some strange coincidence, Mike had played ball on Lambert's baseball team. In another coincidence, Anita had found my husband his first job. This was all before I met Mike.

Anita had a friend named Pete Skouras, who owned the Columns Restaurant in Avon-by-the-Sea, a small town next to Bradley Beach. The Columns featured an elegant hotel with blue-striped awnings and a sweeping wraparound porch. Mike was sixteen, and Anita talked Mr. Skouras into hiring him for the summer. Mike promptly found a job for his friend Warren, and together they spent that summer helping out in the kitchen.

Mike and Warren did well at their new jobs until one fateful summer day. Early that morning, proprietor Pete Skouras had stirred up some hot milk and rice, added eggs and cinnamon, and created his famous Greek rice pudding. Warren, being a robust 6'4" fella', loved good food. He had grown up with the aroma of latkes, challah bread, and borscht, but never tasted anything as delectable as Greek rice pudding. He watched anxiously as Mr. Skouras poured the creamy pudding into a large stainless-steel pan.

"Now put this pudding in the refrigerator to cool," Mr. Skouras ordered, as he disappeared through the swinging doors.

Warren dutifully lifted the heavy pan into the refrigerator. After about half an hour, Warren opened the door to check on the pudding. The scent of cinnamon filled the air like an aphrodisiac.

In the meantime, Mike had left the kitchen and was clearing tables on the porch. Warren looked around, then lifted the heavy tray out of the refrigerator.

"Hmmm," he thought out loud, "smells good. I just think I'll try a little."

Mr. Skouras returned to the kitchen, opened the refrigerator door, and saw an almost empty pan.

"What happened to my rice pudding?"

"I ate it," Warren said sheepishly.

"You ate it! What do you mean you *ate it*?"

"I ate it."

Warren's face blushed a bright red. "There's some left."

"There's not much left," Mr. Skouras shouted. "How could you do this?"

"It was delicious," Warren smiled.

"My rice pudding! What will the customers think?" "You #$%&*!" (In Greek)

Mr. Skouras pointed to the swinging kitchen door. "You're fired! Now get out of here!"

Warren slunk his bulky frame out the door and left. That was the end of his career in the restaurant business. He went on to make millions in the carpet industry. Mike stayed throughout the summer.

When Anita's husband died, she was left to run their restaurant. My father was living on his own in an apartment in Asbury Park. The day my father walked into Anita's restaurant was the beginning of a new relationship. Angy and Anita shared a common heritage, and both spoke Greek. My father acted even more Greek than before. He began to have dinner at The Little Campus during the week and took Anita out on weekends. They began keeping company and soon were accepted in the Greek community as a couple.

Occasionally, they traveled to New York with their friend, Mae, dining at a Greek restaurant, drinking ouzo, and dancing to the bouzouki music to the wee hours of the morning. Sometimes they came home and danced on the hood of Mae's car, parked in front of the restaurant. They seemed happy together. I didn't know what to make of this new romance, so I accepted it.

Anita visited my father's apartment from time to time, and he played Greek music or they listened to his brother Tommy's album. This was the year of the movie *Zorba the Greek*, and my father played the soundtrack over and over. It was one of my father's favorite movies. After a while, he began to identify with Zorba; he thought he *was* Zorba. Ironically, in the movie, Zorba brought his young friend a box of chocolates.

Zorba was the flawed hero with a big heart. He described himself as "stronger than a bull" and asked deep philosophical questions, such as "Why do the young die? Why does anyone die?" To his English friend, he exclaimed: "What's the use of all your damn books? If they don't tell you that, what the hell do they tell you?"

I can still picture my father sitting beside his old record player, playing the soundtrack of his prized album over and over again. I can still hear him dramatizing Zorba's words.

The young man asks Zorba, "Are you married?"

"Am I not a man?" Zorba shouts. "And is not a man stupid?"

"I am a man. So I am married. Wife, children, house, everything—*the full catastrophe*!"

Suddenly the lively tempo of Greek music would float through the apartment and down the hall, accompanied by the rich aroma of roast lamb and potatoes. If you closed your eyes, you could imagine yourself in Greece.

The signal for Angy and Anita to dance was when the young man turned to Zorba and said: "Teach me to dance!"

"Dance, did you say dance? C'mon, my boy!" Zorba beckoned to the young man, and together they began the slow steps of the Sailor's Dance. The movie ends with Zorba and the Englishman dancing happily on the beach.

Zorba tells the young man: "You've got everything but one thing—madness! Man needs a little madness. Without it, he can never break the rope and be free."

Many years later, I realized Zorba was right. My mother's madness *had* set her free.

Anita had a handsome son, Dino. Dino was tall and muscular, with black hair, and eyes as blue as the Aegean Sea. Both his parents being Greek, he looked as if he had just floated down from Mount Olympus. In those days, separation and divorce were not as acceptable in society as they are today. Sometimes it was awkward, but Dino and I realized that our parents had experienced a sense of loneliness and needed some companionship. Years later, I too, would come to understand this same loneliness.

Dino was a quiet, athletic young man who made friends easily. He once had the honor of "catching the cross" on Holy Cross Day in Asbury Park.

On or about the third week in September, at the celebration of the Elevation of the Cross, Father Coutros ceremoniously threw the cross into the ocean alongside Asbury Park's Convention Hall. This ritual honored the day, according to the legend, that Constantine's mother, Helena, found the true cross on a hill in Jerusalem, entwined in a field of sweet-smelling basil.

A select group of young Greek Orthodox boys then dived into the ocean to retrieve the holy cross from the sea. The other boys lifted the victor on their shoulders and carried him up and down the boardwalk like a Greek god. He would be blessed with good fortune for the entire year.

Angy and Anita had a comfortable, long-term relationship for more than twenty years, until a tragedy brought Anita's life to an untimely end. She was visiting a friend's house and mistakenly opened the cellar door and fell down a flight of stairs, dying instantly. Anita had always said that, when she died, she wanted to be surrounded by her family and her friends in the Greek community. Her wishes came true—the entire Greek community came to her funeral. My father was devastated. Over and over, he sobbed, "I loved her, I loved her," as he staggered to his feet.

I began to wonder if there was some kind of curse on my family.

* * *

People with emotional problems tend to be shunned by society. Often, the stigma trickles down to their immediate family.

I heard remarks muttered under people's breath, such as "she's just like her mother," or "the apple doesn't fall far from the tree." When I entered a room, people stopped whispering. I became a target for criticism. One of the women who used to visit our home for dinner suddenly crossed the street to avoid saying hello to me. I came to realize who the phonies of this world were.

When you're down and out, you find out who your true friends are. I tried to understand what was happening to me. My mother had become a stranger and my family had broken apart. Parents who separate and divorce often turn their children against the other parent. My father used that tactic against my mother. I was moving toward adulthood, but totally unprepared for the transition. I wanted answers, and in my quest for answers, I decided that I needed wisdom, so I enrolled in Monmouth College, a small college in the nearby town of West Long Branch. Monmouth College was part of the old Guggenheim Estate, a complex of gracious buildings cropping up along the winding entranceway and rolling lawn. The grounds were lush with oaks, firs, spruce, and cedar trees.

In the middle of the estate stood a great mansion, complete with marble fireplaces, golden friezes, and winding stairs. The mansion featured an indoor swimming pool, outdoor tennis courts, stables, and a carriage house. Marble stairs led to French doors that opened out to a wide verandah. The classes took my mind off the fact that my life had fallen apart. I wanted to study literature and become a writer or teacher.

I signed up for literature, writing, and history classes. When I began my English courses, I was pleasantly surprised. College was a totally different atmosphere from high school. It was much more formal, and the professors didn't tolerate idleness. My history professor wisely cautioned us to "forget everything we learned in high school." Since I never opened a book in high school, that was easy to do.

A whole new world opened up to me. I started studying and doing homework regularly, unlike my practice in high school. I was very quiet in class and didn't talk unless the instructor called on me. We were studying the Rise of Western Civilization, and when the professor noticed that I had a Greek name he called on me the first day.

"Let's see, who will we call on today?" he began.

"Ah, yes, Miss Sakelaris," he continued, looking up from the roster.

"Miss Sakelaris, can you tell us who won the battle of Thermopylae? Was it the Greeks or the Persians?"

I was dumbfounded. I wished I could change my name. My heart did a flip-flop, as the class grew silent. I took a deep breath and gave an answer.

"The Persians," I answered confidently.

"Well, yes. They won the battle, but in a sense, they lost their original mission. When the Persians finally entered Athens, the Greeks had abandoned their city. Did you know that?"

"Well, maybe."

The professor always agreed that the answer was generally acceptable, but in reality—wrong.

He called on me every day. One day he asked me another difficult question.

"I can't answer your question," I sighed. "No matter what answer I give you, you'll prove it's wrong."

Everybody laughed, including the professor.

I was determined to get an education. I persevered and struggled to finish my first semester at Monmouth College.

In early August, with September classes soon to begin, I was working at the candy store. After an argument over my pay, I stormed out of the store and looked for another job.

I walked down the street and stopped in front of the window of an upscale children's store, The Golden Rule. The window display was bright with colorful pleated skirts, button-down cardigans, and pink and blue baby clothes. I walked in the front door.

An elegantly dressed woman behind the counter came to me.

"May I help you?"

"Yes, do you need sales help?"

"Why, yes, we do," she said with a smile. "When can you start?"

"Right now," I replied.

"I'm Esther, what is your name?"

"Joanie Sakelaris. My father has the candy store down the street."

"Oh, yes! I'll take you upstairs and introduce you to the other employees in your department."

The people I met at The Golden Rule were caring, professional individuals. I never worked for Jewish people before, and I was impressed with their positive attitude and problem-solving ability. Not only was the business successful, it kept their family together. Esther was very kind to me. She introduced me to her daughter, a bright young woman. I worked for a while in the teen department upstairs. Esther's daughter befriended me and encouraged me to continue my education. I only worked at The Golden Rule for a short time, but I never forgot Esther and her wonderful family. Esther was a queenly woman. Years later, I read the Biblical story of Esther, and how she saved the Hebrew people from death.

During this time, I lost my faith in God. I stopped attending the Greek Orthodox Church and lost all faith in religion. My friend Suzanne took me to the Catholic Church, and I felt a transitory sense of peace, but I became an agnostic. I wondered why God had abandoned me. I turned to books and philosophy for answers. When I look back, I'm sorry that I turned my back on God. He never turned his back on me. For a long time, I became a cynical young woman. I didn't have a family to celebrate Christmas or Easter with anymore and cynically scoffed at Christmas as a materialistic holiday for hypocrites.

My family was divided by Mother's illness. My father and his brothers acted distant toward me, and many of my old friends drifted away. The embarrassment over my mother's illness was making me a loner. I began to feel like an invisible person. I wanted to hide from people and hide from life. My old life and dreams, along with my idealism, were fading away. Disorder and discord threatened me, and I couldn't find peace and harmony anywhere. Maybe this sounds paranoid, but I didn't know where to turn, or who to trust any more. Reading gave me a sense of solace.

In his book, *Invisible Man*, Ralph Ellison writes:

> Deep down you come to suspect that you yourself are to blame, and you stand naked

> and shivering before the millions of eyes who
> look through you unseeingly.

Now I really felt alone. My friend Suzanne had married Bob, a wealthy, older man. Bob was good to her, and she happily settled down in her new life. I didn't want to live alone, so I went to live with my grandmother, in Bradley Beach. While attending college, I met a nice young man, Larry Dooley, who often gave me a ride to school. I also met Norman Konvitz, who took me to the Paper Mill Playhouse, and Trader Vic's in New York City. Norman was a wonderful, caring young man.

My grandmother always told me that I should have married him, and she was right. Norman was Jewish, and he even took me home to meet his parents.

"Mom, Dad, this is Joanie Sakelaris," he announced proudly.

They smiled politely, but I think inside they were saying "*Oy vey.*"

"Uh, oh," I thought to myself. This is going to be a clash of cultures, just like my parents' relationship. What would I bring to the relationship? I was embarrassed by my mother's illness and my parents' ugly separation. My mother had taken to spending wildly and acting irrationally. I remembered how my mother tried to throw an ironing board at me. I think she had a point. I took this as a sign that I should never waste my time ironing.

How could I introduce Norman's family to my mother? I didn't think they would understand. Even I didn't understand anymore. No, it wouldn't work. To this day, I still have wonderful memories of Norman, and regrets, too.

So, I ran back to Mike. Mike was my security blanket. I always thought he was stronger than I was. One night, about five months after we broke up, my friend Donna and I were walking along the Asbury Park beachfront. Mike and his friend Richie drove by and spotted us.

"Stop the car!" I heard Mike yell.

"If you talk to her, I'll leave you here!" Richie shouted as he pulled his big gray Cadillac to the curb.

Mike hopped out of the car, and Richie drove away. Mike and I made up that night.

About twenty-five years later, as Mike and I were riding down Florida's Route A1A in Richie's white Rolls Royce Corniche, I couldn't help remembering that night. The sun was warm against my skin, and the wind was blowing through my hair. As I ran my fingers over the soft leather upholstery, I shook my head in amazement.

"I can't believe I'm riding through Boca Raton in a Rolls Royce with you and Richie!"

Life just seems to happen to me. Over twenty years had gone by. It was as though nothing had changed, and yet everything had changed. Richie had become fabulously wealthy, but inside he was still just Mike's buddy. He hadn't changed much physically. He had the same sparkling blue eyes, wavy blonde hair, and Irish wit he had when he was young.

That was the umpteenth time Mike and I made up, and he started visiting me at my grandmother's house. Gran was not too keen on Mike, and she made her dislike evident. Once when I announced that Mike was coming over, "Gran puffed her chest out and stomped around the living room muttering, "Mussolini, Mussolini."

"Very funny, Gran."

If I asked if Mike could come over for cake and coffee, Gran would say, "Yes, he's wasting away to a ton."

Mike was working for Drake's Cakes at the time, delivering snack cakes and pies to local restaurants. He tried to win Gran over with raisin bread, pecan rolls, and mini fruit pies, but she just nodded and hid the loot in the kitchen. Her only concession to Mike was offering him a cup of her treasured A&P coffee.

28

It was November 22, 1963. I was living with my grandmother in Bradley Beach while I attended Monmouth College. The Beatles had taken the world by storm. "I Want to Hold Your Hand" was number three on the charts, and Roy Orbison's "In Dreams" was in the top forty.

I had gone upstairs and sprawled out on my grandmother's old four-poster bed to study my literature homework. I was reading poems from Wordsworth's "Ode: Intimations on Immortality." One passage really struck me:

> Though nothing can bring back the hour,
> Of splendor in the grass, of glory in the flower,
> We will grieve not, rather find,
> Strength in what remains behind.

I closed the book. The indistinguishable hum of the TV drifted upstairs. The house was as cold as a sepulcher. I snuggled under the thick down comforter until I drifted off to sleep. As my head rested on the feather pillow, I found myself immersed in the middle of a strange dream. The dream was so real, so vivid, as though I had gone back in time.

The dream, framed in black and white, unfolded slowly. I was standing along the parade route on Pennsylvania Avenue, Washington, DC. I was wearing a dark gray dress and jacket. The crowd was weeping and sobbing. I heard the slow beating of the drums and watched as six white horses pulled a wagon down the avenue. The horses shook their feathered plumes restlessly as the air echoed with the clippety-clop of horses' hooves and the rumble of wagon wheels. A funeral procession was passing by. A gust of wind rippled over the flag-draped coffin.

"Who is it?" I whispered to the oddly dressed woman next to me.

"Why, don't you know? It's our president—President Lincoln! He's been assassinated!"

"The president?" I responded. "It can't be! It's 1963! Kennedy is president."

"Kennedy? You must be crazy; there's no president with that name. It's President *Lincoln*!" she hissed, her eyes shooting me a dark, wild look.

"President Lincoln has been shot!"

The pale horses passed by. The crowd stood silent as the drums rolled, and the woman's voice faded into a drumbeat.

The dream was so intense that I could smell the musky scent of the horses and feel their steamy breath. As the coffin passed before me, I felt a sense of dread. I was rooted to the ground, but the drums kept beating and the procession kept moving. A black riderless stallion followed, its stirrups facing backwards to signify the fallen warrior. Slowly, the drums began to echo and fade down the hallway of broken dreams.

I tossed and turned, uneasy with the strange dream. Suddenly the volume of the television grew louder and drifted up the stairs. I awoke fitfully and shook my head in disbelief.

"What a crazy dream," I thought to myself as I yawned and rubbed the sleep from my eyes. I threw on a sweater and padded down the stairs on my well-worn slippers. Gran was sitting quietly in front of the TV, her arms crossed over her chest and her face as solemn as a headstone. She had turned the volume up. I plopped down on the overstuffed sofa.

"Why is the TV so loud?" I asked. "What happened?"

Gran fixed me with her watery blue eyes and announced, "The president's just been shot."

"*What*!" I cried. "The president? President Kennedy? *No*! That's impossible!"

I thought of my dream. Why was I dreaming of President Lincoln's assassination? Nothing made sense.

The news stated that President Kennedy had been shot outside the Texas School Book Depository while traveling in a presidential motorcade. The president had been rushed to nearby Dallas Hospital. Reporters and bystanders had gathered at the hospital for the latest information, and bystanders were screaming and weeping in the streets. The tears were streaming down their faces.

Time stood still as we waited for the news. I had a bad feeling in my stomach, which, by now, was rumbling. I kept thinking of my dream.

We waited for what seemed like an hour. Suddenly, a news bulletin flashed across the screen. Walter Cronkite, the renowned newscaster, appeared on the screen.

"President Kennedy died today . . . at 1:00 PM Central Time, 2:00 PM Eastern Standard Time, some thirty-eight minutes ago."

Mr. Cronkite looked at the clock, cleared his throat, and removed his black-rimmed glasses.

"Excuse me," he continued, brushing away tears.

My grandmother and I sat together in stunned silence.

John Fitzgerald Kennedy, the 35th President of the United States and America's youngest elected president, was dead. Forty-three years old, Kennedy was the embodiment of a youthful generation, having proclaimed "that the torch has been passed to a new generation of Americans."

I thought of President Kennedy's inaugural address and that memorable quote: "Ask not what your country can do for you, but what *you* can do for your country."

John Kennedy called his new administration the New Frontier. He led the United States through the fiasco of the Bay of Pigs invasion, the tense 1962 Cuban missile crisis, and the American Civil Rights Movement. In Germany, he wowed the public with his famous "*Ich bin ein Berliner*" speech. Kennedy encouraged America toward excellence. He appealed to young people to volunteer and join the Peace Corps. President Kennedy promoted space exploration and anticipated man landing on the moon. When he traveled to Paris with his wife Jacqueline, he described himself as the "man who accompanied Jackie Kennedy to France."

Our president was dead. Now, like Lincoln, he belonged to the ages.

My grandmother was silent.

"This can't be happening!" I blurted out.

I was only nineteen years old. These things only happened in history books, not in *my* generation. This was the 20th

Century. It was unthinkable. I had read about the assassinations of Lincoln, McKinley, and Archduke Ferdinand, but they happened many years ago. Things like that didn't happen anymore, not to young, popular, vibrant men. Yet, it had happened, now. It wasn't past history. It wasn't a dream. It was reality.

I thought of the President's beautiful wife, the elegant Jackie Kennedy. A-line dresses and white pearls revealed the signature style of a classic beauty. She set the style for a new generation. Jackie was just as lovely in dark slacks and white blouse as in her inaugural gown. I thought of her soft voice, as she guided viewers through a televised tour of the White House. I thought of her endearing children, Caroline and John-John. I remembered pictures of Caroline atop her pony, "Macaroni," and I thought of the photo of little John-John, playing under his father's desk in the Oval Office.

What kind of madman would want to kill the president? Why? Everything was going wrong, not only in my life, but also in my country.

The sun was fading, and the news droned on. A suspect, Lee Harvey Oswald, had been captured as a suspect. Oswald was whisked off to the Dallas County jail. Meanwhile, Jackie, still wearing her pink, blood-spattered, suit, had placed her wedding ring on her husband's hand.

"Let them see what they have done," she was rumored to have said.

My grandmother and I sat together in silence. I had believed in my God, my family, and my government. I depended on them and held them in high esteem. My world was shattered. Everything I believed in was falling apart. My grandmother didn't have a phone, so we couldn't call anyone. Television had brought the drama into our homes. Unless you were watching television or listening to the radio, you didn't know what was happening. A great silence encircled us. There we were an old woman and a young girl trapped in an uncertain future.

We heard a knock at the door. It was Mike. He had been delivering cake and bread in Asbury Park when he heard the sad news from one of his customers. He confessed that he had been crying. He said that people were weeping and mourning in the streets. We sat together in stunned silence, staring into the television.

The next day, the headlines showed the historic photograph of the swearing in of Lyndon Johnson while a grieving Jackie Kennedy looked on. The news showed President Kennedy's body being transported back to Washington for the funeral.

The following days were full of sadness and drama. No author could have contrived such a plot. On November 22, Lee Harvey Oswald was questioned in the death of President Kennedy. Oswald was portrayed as a malcontent who had once lived in the Soviet Union for a short time. On the morning of November 24, as Oswald was being transferred from the Dallas County jail, nightclub owner Jack Ruby shot and killed Oswald. A cameraman was filming the transfer live, when suddenly Jack Ruby lunged forward, fired a gun point blank, and shot Oswald. We watched the shooting live on television.

"He's been shot, he's been shot, Lee Oswald has been shot!" a reporter shouted. Later, Jack Ruby rationalized his actions.

"This man killed my president," Ruby stated angrily.

Now Oswald was dead, too.

Monday, November 25, 1963 dawned with an eerie silence. Mourners filed through the Capitol rotunda to pay their last respects to the president. In Washington, the morning air echoed with the beat of muffled drums and the steady clip-clop of six white horses. A spirited black stallion, chafing at the handler's bit, pranced behind the coffin. The riderless horse tossed his spirited head, as its nostrils filled the air with short bursts of steam.

The President's little son, John-John, saluted his father's final journey as the procession passed by. Jacqueline Kennedy, dressed in a simple black suit and veil, held Caroline's hand. Television had brought the tragedy into our living room. Mourners lined the sides of Pennsylvania Avenue as the Kennedy clan, flanking Jackie, marched behind the coffin. The drums beat slowly. People were sobbing. A thin black veil shaded Jackie's dark eyes and soft features. Once in a while, the camera caught her anguish beneath the shadows.

My grandmother and I sat quietly. Not a car went by. There wasn't a sound to be heard. Nothing. The shopkeepers closed their doors for the day. Many shops placed photos of President Kennedy in their windows in memoriam. The day unfolded like a Greek tragedy. Even my father closed the candy store as a sign of respect.

President Kennedy was buried at Arlington National Cemetery. An Eternal Flame was lit in his memory. Our dreams of a New Frontier and Camelot were shattered, a pall descended on the country.

Jackie Kennedy had planned her husband's funeral to resemble the funeral of Abraham Lincoln. The effect was solemn, but stately. All eyes were upon Mrs. Kennedy during the service. Her grace and strength gave us hope during the darkest days. How I admired Jackie's courage—I don't know how she stood up to such a sudden catastrophe. She wasn't just another fashion plate, but a strong woman of character. I could only imagine the depths of her sorrow. I didn't think I could ever be that strong.

I wasn't the only person living in a world of anxiety. Everything seemed to stand still. The country stood still. My life stood still. God stood still. There was no Thanksgiving that year for me. Gran and I ate grilled-cheese sandwiches in front of the TV that day. I wonder if many other families did the same. I felt depressed, as if nothing mattered any more. It was the same sense of emptiness I felt after my mother's breakdown.

I wish I could say that I turned to God and prayer, but I didn't see any future in my life. I continued reading, studying, and looking for answers. Books were always a sense of solace and escape for me. Unfortunately, I neglected to read the most inspirational book of all—the Bible.

Something in me changed after the assassination of President Kennedy. I thought of his famous words: "The hope still lives, and the dream shall never die." What of his dream now? What would happen to his promise for the space

program? President Kennedy believed that "this nation should commit itself to achieving the goal before the decade is out, of landing a man on the moon and returning him safely to Earth. No single space project in this period will be more impressive to mankind or more important for the long-range exploration of space."

Would America ever land a man on the moon?

I wondered how *I* would be remembered after I was gone. I struggled to find meaning in my life and wondered about my own mortality. Fear of dying alone overwhelmed me. I was disillusioned with materialism and the struggle for success. I turned more and more to Mike for emotional support. I was still working in the candy store, but I felt more like an employee than a member of the family. Deep down inside, I wanted to have a family of my own.

29

Christmas came and went that year. I hardly remember it. On Christmas Eve I bought Gran a scraggly little tree. We tried to make the most of the holiday, no matter what was happening in the world and in our lives. I wish I could say I celebrated the religious aspect of the holiday, but my faith was gone. Gran went to visit Uncle Wilbur and Aunt Julie for New Year's, and I was alone. Mike came to visit, but I wasn't much company.

Gran never said much about my mother being sick. Our loved one's illness had changed our lives. We were caught in the middle. It was Gran's daughter who was sick, but she was also my mother. Sometimes I think we both felt as though we had failed respectively as mother and daughter. I tried to be a good daughter, but my mother pushed me away. Gran never discussed my mother's illness; it was as though she was hiding some dark secret.

The drab days of winter faded, giving birth to the bright days of spring. One afternoon, there was a knock on the door. I peeked out the window and saw my mother standing at the door. Her face was in a scowl and furrows crept across her forehead. Her yellow slacks fell loosely over her scuffed white flats. I hadn't seen my mother since September. She looked angry, but Gran opened the door anyway. We never did find out how she got there unless she walked the three miles from home to Bradley Beach.

Gran quietly opened the front door and let my mother in.

My mother stood there with clenched fists. Her pale eyes darted about the room.

"Where are my things?" Mother shouted.

"Your things? What things?" Gran asked. "Marjorie, all your things are in your house, in Interlaken."

"No! My things are here! You took them. You took them all, my China, my coats, my jewelry!" Mother shouted, clenching her fists.

"Margie, calm down. I don't have your things. I have no room here for them. See for yourself," Gran assured her.

"They're upstairs! I know they're upstairs!" Mother shouted, then clambered up the rickety stairs that led to the bedroom.

I followed, but she didn't seem to notice me. I felt as if I had been given a veil of invisibility. Mother began rifling through the drawers, throwing scarves, nighties, and intimate apparel aside. Suddenly, she lifted an antique bracelet high in the air.

"Here it is! My gold bracelet! You had it all the time. You stole it!" she shouted down the stairs.

I was incredulous. It was *Gran's* bracelet. Once Gran had shown me the inscription, *A.M.M.* [Aimee Marie Miller]. The bracelet even had a tiny dent in it.

Mother scooped up the bracelet and slipped it into her pocket. She turned and faced the stairs. I heard the clacking of her flats as she hurried down the steps. All the while she looked at me as if I wasn't there. My mother didn't even know who I was!

I stood there, looking at my refection in the mirror. It had blended with my mother's, and I wondered if our spirits were imprisoned together in the mirror. I ran down the stairs just in time to hear the door slam. My mother was gone as quickly as she came. She didn't even say goodbye.

Gran sat on the sofa, her eyes wet with tears. I had never seen her cry. Never.

"Gran! You're crying!" I wailed. "What's wrong?"

"It's all my fault!" she wept, brushing away tears. "I never told you this, but your mother's father abandoned us when she was a little girl. He moved around the corner with his mistress. We were destitute, and your Uncle Wilbur had to quit school to support us. Uncle Bobby worked at the vegetable store around the corner. Your grandfather died from blood poisoning while painting a neighbor's garage roof; he fell and scraped his hands on the shingles.

"When your grandfather died the men from the fire company knocked on the front door and shouted, 'Your husband is dead; your husband is dead!' Then they left. We were on relief—no one helped us. We had no heat, very little food, and it was so cold, so cold. My own family forgot me."

I slumped down on the sofa. I had never noticed how scratchy the material was.

"Don't blame yourself, Gran," I sighed, hugging her. "It was your husband's fault, not yours. He was the one that left. You did your best."

"He forgot us; everyone forgot us. Now your mother is sick," she sniffed.

I handed her a tissue.

"Why didn't you tell me the truth years ago?" I sighed.

"I wanted to protect you."

"Lies do not protect people."

"I'm sorry, I'm sorry. I thought I was protecting you."

Right then and there, I vowed that I would never withhold the truth about anything from *my* children. (I would live to eat my words.)

Gran dabbed her eyes. "I think I'll make some coffee," she said, composing herself.

Crestfallen, I sat there, stunned. How could my grandmother have lied to me? My grandfather didn't die of a heart attack at all!

There was no hope for my family. Now I knew the truth. No wonder my mother had emotional problems. Now I knew why I never saw any photos of Gran's family as a family. I don't even have a photo of my mother when she was a child, only photos of her as a teenager. I don't even know where my grandfather is buried. This was the well-guarded family secret. One man's irresponsibility had trickled down to the second generation. I clenched my fists in anger. Resentment welled up within me like bile. Maybe it was time to start a family of my own—I didn't want to be alone and unloved for the rest of my life.

30

At this time, I had a friend named Donna. Donna and I had met at Bond Street Grammar School and attended Asbury Park High School together. Donna was a lively, loyal friend. Her nickname was "Bouncer," not because she worked in a bar, but because she bounced when she walked. Donna was tall, slender, and cute. I can still picture her dark ponytail flipping from side to side as she bounced down the hall toward the school's auditorium. Donna was the clean cut, preppy, girl-next-door type. She had an infectious laugh, bright smile, and upbeat personality.

Whenever my friends and I had a problem, we turned to Donna, our Mother Superior. (Remember, I'm not in any way insinuating that my friends and I were nuns.) Donna was always realistic, while I was a quixotic blonde. Known for her lectures concerning the pitfalls of puppy love, she advised us to guard our emotions and our bodies from the snares of infatuation. Donna warned us that men set snares for us, and innocent young ladies that we were, we must protect ourselves from the bestial attacks of these amorous young men.

Donna really did give good advice. We were convinced that Donna never did anything wrong, and that she was a cold fish who would end up married to an accountant or college professor.

She attracted nice preppy guys—the local WASPs. She surprised us all by marrying Sal, a vibrant, hardworking man who once stripped down to his red skivvies while dancing to the song "Macho Man." I never did understand how Donna's marriage outlasted most of our marriages.

Everyone has a friend like Donna, a friend who tells you the right thing to do, and when you listen to that friend, you ruin your life forever. Of course, the Donnas in this world mean well. They do have all the right answers, but in the end, when you listen to them, they mess you up. Donna reminded me that I had been going out with Mike for about four years. She hinted that people *might talk* because Mike hadn't proposed yet. (Looking back, this statement sounds hilarious.) Maybe Mike needed to protect himself from me.

Donna suggested that if Mike was really serious, he should officially propose. This, of course, entailed buying an engagement ring. The theory behind this was that, not only could I show off the ring, I would become an honest woman. I think Mother Superior was either planning my wedding or my funeral.

Donna was always a great person and a faithful friend. How could I not listen to the voice of success? Why not? Because their advice only works for them! *You* are a different person, with different needs. Your life becomes a series of catastrophes, while your friend spends the rest of his or her life wearing beautiful clothes, wintering in Florida, and giving advice that only works in her world.

Mother Superior coached me on how to behave if I wanted a guy to give me presents.

"Play hard to get," Donna whispered. "You know, no hugging, no kissing, well, you know what I mean," she lectured.

"You mean I shouldn't go parking anymore? Who are you trying to punish—me or Mike?"

"Oh, don't be so silly," Donna clucked like a mother hen, shaking her head, "do you want people to talk about you?"

"I really don't care. My life is in shambles anyway. My mother has lost her mind, my father worries about how I put candy in boxes, and I just lost my other job as a waitress. What else could happen to me?" I anguished. If I could only have seen the future. (I should have been the runaway bride, or maybe my husband should have been the runaway husband.)

"Take my advice. It's time Mike made an honest woman of you."

I listened to Donna. I played hard to get. It worked! It was August of 1964. Mike surprised me with a lovely marquise engagement ring for my birthday. I was ecstatic! I don't know where Mike got the money; he must have paid for the ring on time. A proposal and an engagement ring—the romance was electrifying. The problem was that Mike and I were not ready for marriage.

How could I be a good wife? I didn't know how to cook, sew, or take care of babies. At least Mike had a job. He looked and acted so much older than I was. Of course, it was true that we were attracted to each other and made a nice couple. Mike's dark muscular presence complimented my skinny legs and sleek blonde pageboy.

Mike and I married on October 24, 1964, four days before Halloween. How appropriate; the significance is noteworthy. It was a lovely wedding, or should I say forced elopement? Our friends had plied Mike with liquor and threw him in the back seat of the car. Mike's friend Skippy propped Mike up at the altar. Neither the Greek Church nor the Catholic Church would perform the ceremony unless one of us converted to the other's religion. Luckily, we found a minister who would marry us. We were finally married at Ballard Methodist Church in Asbury Park. The minister assured us that "No one I ever married has been divorced." (I wonder if he was actually referring to *his* wife.)

My new husband was so soused he could hardly stand up, and I wanted to catch the next stage out of town. It was Indian summer, and my white wool dress made my skin itch. I was twenty years old; Mike was almost twenty-three. I never walked well in high heels, and stumbled down the aisle. We stood at the altar and vowed to take each other "in sickness and in health, 'til death do us part." I took my vows seriously, but no one thought our marriage would last.

It was a marriage of passion, struggle, love, anger, and resentment. We were both young and temperamental. Our families were dysfunctional. Our mothers, who had been full of promise, became institutionalized in the same hospital only a few months apart. We were high-school sweethearts gone wrong.

For a long time, I was a bitter young woman. I turned my back on God. Mike wasn't a saint, and neither was I, but I tried my best to keep my family together. Mike and I were married, and it wasn't easy; we struggled financially, and Mike often worked two jobs to support us. I had no skills, and no income whatsoever. We had very little. My tiara had tarnished.

Mike was a handsome, hardworking, and charismatic man. For a while, we lived in Red Bank and Mike waited on tables at Sal's Tavern. Mike had an eye for the ladies. Some of his friends described him as a "prince," but I thought of him as the "prince of darkness."

When I first got married, true to my father's predictions, I didn't know how to make a meal. My idea of making spaghetti sauce was emptying a bottle of ketchup into a pot and adding a bottle of water. More than anything, I wanted to have a baby. I wanted to have a home and a loving family. My dreams were realized when I had a beautiful baby girl. I named her Lori. I didn't know how to change a diaper; the first time I tried, I threw up! My friends had to come and help me. I gained thirty pounds with my first baby, and Mike nicknamed me "Buddha."

We had nothing. I kept my baby in a dresser drawer until Mike's Aunt Faye gave me a baby shower and a bassinet. We had little food, no car, and no insurance. We were a mess.

I was useless—totally unprepared for marriage and motherhood. However, I slowly began to change. My father taught me to cook, something I never wanted to do, and I even learned how to clean the house. Like many young girls, my dreams of love and marriage were unrealistic. A successful marriage requires a lot of hard work, sacrifice, and patience. My husband and I just couldn't get it right. Our marriage was no bed of roses—it was more like a thicket of blackberries.

I'll never know what magnetic force brings ordinary people together in body, mind, and spirit. Is it fate? We are joined for better or worse—sometimes better, sometimes worse. We seek to love this person and mold them to our oneness. Do we ever really *love* this person, or merely the illusion that person possesses?

Only when our loved one is stripped of that illusion can we truly love them, the true essence, and the true spirit God has revealed to us. The deepest love can overwhelm us when we see our loved one reaching out to us, grasping at life. We see a corner of their soul that was forever hidden from us, obscured by ego. We know that there is a secret place within us that houses our soul. God has given great power to the sick, for in their weakness, we glimpse some deep truth, not only of their suffering, but the suffering of all humanity.

My marriage became a tempestuous repository for sadness, joy, and personal growth. Why do we chase the façade of another human being? Within two-and-a-half years, I had a handsome little boy, Michael. I loved my children and tried my best to raise them right. They gave me a sense of purpose and a reason to live. Having children eased my loneliness. They were good kids, made friends easily, and enjoyed growing up at the Jersey Shore. However, I began to realize how difficult it was to be a parent. In fact, it was downright scary.

I wanted to make up for all the hurt I experienced in my parents' breakup, but instead, both my husband and I experienced more hurt. We didn't have any money. We fought like cats and dogs, but somehow, we always made up. It's sad how the promise of youth can turn to disappointment. How we wasted our youth, our energy, and our potential.

I beseech you, be you a husband, wife, or lover—don't let this happen to you. Don't become preoccupied with the meaningless activities of life. Don't let ego drive your anger until you and your loved one are looking at each other across that courtroom, emergency room, or nursing home wondering, "What happened to *us*?"

I speak from experience. I really got to know my husband when he became sick in his mid-forties. First, he was injured on the job. Later, his health declined until his hands shook and he had difficulty walking. By the time he was forty-seven, he couldn't even run his cake route anymore. When he was fifty-two, he had a stroke and was admitted into a nursing home. He died, sixty years old, in the nursing home, where I visited him almost every day.

My husband delivered bread and baked goods for Bond Bread and Hostess Cake. One thing about Mike, he always was a hard worker. His work was the love of his life, and he never missed a day working on the trucks. One January he left the house at 2:30 in a blizzard, only to return when he learned the Garden State Parkway was closed due to the storm.

He stood before me, wet snow dropping on the kitchen floor.

"I told you not to go to go to work in this weather!" I reprimanded him.

"That's my job, to deliver the bread."

This reminds me of the Saint Patrick's Day when the police called me around dusk.

"Mrs. Corcione?" the officer asked politely.

"Yes? I'm Mrs. Corcione."

"Are you missing a husband?'

"I wanted to say, 'I hope so,' but I bit my tongue.

"Why?" I asked.

"We just found him parked on the tennis court singing Irish songs."

"Uh, oh. What are you going to do, officer?"

"Well, he's OK, but he said he stopped for a few drinks on his way home from work, and he didn't want to drive. Looks like he's a hard-working guy."

"That's for sure—not a lazy bone in his body."

"Well, it *is* St. Patty's Day," the policeman assured me.

"Yes, officer, and he's half Irish."

"We'll sober him up and send him home."

Mike had charmed his way out of that one, too. He came home three hours later, full of himself.

Marriage was a struggle. Tommy and Neil, my husband's uncles, helped Mike get a job as a route driver in the bakery business. Somehow, we managed to purchase an old house on Princeton Avenue in Brick Town, New Jersey, on the VA plan for $15,400. I had saved a whopping $300 for a down payment. With its bungalow-style white stucco exterior and emerald-green shutters, the house resembled an Irish cottage. It turned out to be a real fixer-upper. The original owner had built the house himself, including the bathroom around the bathtub. Every day was another catastrophe. The septic system collapsed, and we didn't even have a washing machine.

The underground spring beneath the house regularly flooded the basement, the plumbing was patched with duct tape, and our "furnace" was a simple kerosene burner. The only thing that didn't leak was the roof. But the area was beautiful and tranquil.

Brick Town in the early 1970's was a sleepy shore town of scrub pines, colonial-ranch-style homes, and summer cottages. Brick had all the local color of a seashore town on the rise. We lived across the street from the Metedeconk River. The woods were full of narrow footpaths that wound through farms, hidden tree forts, and bushes teeming with wild blueberries. Our cottage stood on a slight hill across from the river. My children grew and flourished in this shore atmosphere; they went exploring in the spring, sledding in the winter, and crabbing in the spring.

My husband always brought home junk cars. He said they saved him money in the long run, but they actually cost more money. I had an old, dilapidated station wagon that ran well, but the floor was sinking and there was a hole in the floor where you could see the road.

Well, it just happens that New Jersey has car inspections, and my car was due for the dreaded trip to the inspection station. Since my neighbor's luxury Cadillac just failed inspection, I had to find a way to make sure my clunker passes the test.

It was July and the weather was hot and sunny, a perfect beach day. I slipped into my new royal-blue bathing suit, sandals, and flimsy cover up, then loaded the kids into the car. A week before, I had placed two stickers on the bumper, one said "Ireland," and the other "Italy."

"OK, kids! We're heading to the beach, but we're making a short stop to get the car inspected," I chirped.

The kids groaned, but off we went.

I drove to Toms River and got in line. It was early, so the line was short. I drove up to the first stop sign, stepped out of the car with the children, and stood on the walkway. Heads turned to the "click, click, click" of my sandals as I sashayed down to the waiting area.

While waiting, my head high, basking in my cleverness, the attendant tested the lights and wipers, then drove the car across the ramp. We heard a loud "scre-eech" when he slammed on the brakes.

As I approached the exit booth, I gave the attendant a big smile and waited patiently to see if I passed. He smiled back and slapped a passing sticker on the old jalopy. I thanked him, wiggled over to the car, gathered my children, and drove away.

31

I believe that God sends us angels in the form of friends. God sent me some wonderful new friends: Cookie, Ann, Ida, Fokiko, and Pat. In the summer, Cookie took her children and mine to the beach. My friends and I laughed and cried together as we watched our children grow.

Cookie changed my life forever when she invited me to a prayer meeting. I had never experienced a prayer meeting, and it promised to be an exciting experience. Cookie, Pat, and my new friends led me to the Lord, and, in 1973, I accepted Jesus Christ as my personal savior. My friends invited me to join their neighborhood Bible study at Joann Stech's house. For years I had resisted God, but God wrestled me back to Him. The charismatic movement was sweeping the country, and I was eager to become a part of it. At that time, I was still confused about my life. I needed peace.

I discovered a tiny Orthodox church in Brick Town that had been converted from a garage. The church was more like a small chapel. Plain wood paneling and a rough, hand carved iconostasis framed the altar. Folding chairs and a worn linoleum floor welcomed the faithful parishioners. Nevertheless, the Orthodox Church of the Annunciation became a refuge in my time of spiritual and emotional need.

Most of the parishioners were Czechoslovakian, Russian, and Ukrainian, but there were also Greeks and converts to the

Orthodox faith. I was introduced to a new culture that featured pierogies, kielbasa, and babka. Father Joseph Wargo was the priest at the time, and he welcomed all nationalities. I honored the various traditions and addressed the priest's wife as "Matushka." The acceptance of all nationalities and converts, and the humility of the congregation, impressed me.

The church has blossomed into a magnificent Byzantine-styled edifice with a large congregation. I'm proud to say that I was there, over thirty-five years ago, shortly after the church began.

My new friends became my support group. They became strong role models for me to follow—I wanted to emulate them. They had lovely homes and successful marriages. My marriage, however, was tough. My husband liked fast women and slow horses. We struggled financially and emotionally and fought constantly. Many weekends found me alone.

I found peace and salvation in my new life. My friends invited me to their local Bible Study, and my journey had begun. I remember the words to one of the first songs I learned: "I have decided to follow Jesus, no turning back, no turning back."

I've been on that journey ever since.

During the charismatic meetings, I was encouraged to pray for healing. I began to pray for my mother. I was in my early thirties then, and my mother had been sick for fifteen years.

Within two months, my prayers were miraculously answered—my mother's condition improved. In six months, she had overcome her debilitating agoraphobia and slowly began venturing out of the house. Her socialization helped her to grow stronger and fight back feelings of depression.

I watched as a new woman emerged from the ashes. The transformation was miraculous. Like the Phoenix, my mother drew strength by reinventing herself. I kept praying, and little by little, my mother showed a marked improvement. I began visiting her more often and brought my children, even feeling confident enough to leave them in her care.

Lori was eleven years old, and Michael was eight. They gave my mother a purpose. She was wonderful to them, and they spent delightful summers at her home. My children continue to speak lovingly of their grandmother.

I don't know if my mother purposely tried to right the wrongs our family had suffered. Sometimes I honestly believe that my mother, having redeemed and found her true self, was a better mother than me.

It seemed inconceivable that an irreverent, confused person like me could have grown so much spiritually and emotionally. I was doubtful, angry, and headstrong. Even today, I keep falling, but God lifts me up again. Sometimes I feel so strong in my faith, and sometimes I feel so small and insignificant, just like Alice in Wonderland when she drank the shrinking potion. I know that I still have a long way to go.

32

One of the happiest times in my life was in 1976, when Mike won a ten-day trip to Italy. As a route driver for Bond Bread, when he sold a certain large number of loaves of bread, he earned a raffle ticket for a trip to Italy. Lori and Michael had filled out about fifty tickets with Mike's name on them, and Mike's ticket was picked from the drum!

Mike and I flew to Rome with a group of owners, friends, and contest winners. We arrived in Rome the week before Palm Sunday and spent a week in the Eternal City.

Rome was a romantic, pulsating city of ancient edifices, magnificent artwork, and culture. A city of gold. We stayed at a posh hotel on the Via Cavour, one of the large, main avenues. The floors were mottled gray and white marble, and the bathroom featured gilt mirrors and gold-plated fixtures. St. Peter's Basilica, the Vatican Museum, and the Sistine Chapel were the highlights of our trip.

When members of our tour group each paid $10 to visit the Vatican, we were told that all we had to do was hop a trolley and walk right in the front door of St. Peter's, so we hopped on a trolley, paid our twenty-five cents, and arrived at St. Peter's just in time to see the Papal Mass.

Miraculously, the Holy Door was open to all pilgrims in celebration of the year of Jubilee. Mike and I took our seats by the aisle in a pew right up front. We bowed our heads in reverence as the bearers carried Pope Paul VI down the aisle on his papal chair, right in front of us. As the Pope brushed by us, we could almost reach out and touch his robe. We sat reverently, awed by the pageantry, the sweeping altar, and the magnificence of Bernini's ebony columns.

After the sacred mass, we filed down the aisle. As we neared the back of the Basilica, we were surprised to see members of our tour group standing in the corner. They waved to us and asked how we had managed to sit up front.

We waved back and shouted, "We just hopped the trolley! It only cost us twenty-five cents!" We may have been the poorest couple on the trip, but from then on, the others regarded us with respect.

Mike knew a lot about history; history was his hobby. He read biographies, books on the Second World War, and Oriental history, such as Frank Clavell's *Shogun*. He was smart. Regrettably, Mike never finished college. He could have done much more with his life, rather than waste his energy and youth drinking, gambling, and running around with women.

I'm no saint either, but I keep trying. Passion brought us together, and passion destroyed us, but when we were in Italy, two genuine people emerged. The facades fell away in the hushed quiet of the Coliseum and under the stars of Rome. It was almost as though Mike and I had finally come home. We enjoyed the lull of tranquility—visiting the galleries, churches, and quaint cafes.

In the afternoon, shopkeepers rolled down their awnings and closed for a few hours. Mike and I fell into the tradition of stopping by a local fruit vendor or bakery and then slipping into our room for an afternoon *pisolino*. We left our struggles and battles behind. Italy was the honeymoon we never had; we strolled the narrow streets, savored the warm Italian food, and took *pisolinos* in the middle of the day. If only our married life could be like it was in Italy—the wine, the music, and the romance of Rome. It was like when we were young. There were no interfering relatives throwing our parent's mistakes in our faces, no bill collectors, and no housework. Maybe we should have moved to Italy and become first-generation immigrants in reverse.

The Coliseum gave me an eerie feeling. When we stood together among the ruins, Mike looked up at the blue sky, turned to me and said, "I feel as though I've been here before."

We tossed pennies in the Trevi Fountain, and as they sank to the bottom, we made a wish that someday we would return. At night, we hitched a tour bus into the hills and watched Rome beneath the stars. We took side trips to Naples and the lost city of Pompeii. Our bus tour found us enjoying fresh seafood by the Bay of Naples, holding on to our seats as we lurched above the winding cliffs of Amalfi Drive, while listening to the bus driver crooning Italian love songs.

Ah! Naples. "*Regina Mare*," the very name evokes the little town by the sea. Thank goodness we were warned not to drink the strong wine of Naples; some of the tourists didn't heed the warning and became woozy.

Our tour guide led us through Pompeii and the dead silence of a doomed city. We were overwhelmed by feelings of our own mortality. On August 24th AD 79, Mount Vesuvius erupted, trapping and killing most of the inhabitants with smoke and ash. Those who could escape fled to the sea.

I wondered what the inhabitants were doing when they died. What were they thinking? Did the victims die regretting things they had done, or not done? Just as they opened their eyes to the fragility of life—they were blinded by death.

As we walked along the ruins the slap of my sandals echoed down the cobblestones of centuries. I was uncomfortable. All was still—not even a bird sang in Pompeii. We marveled at the remains of an ancient temple, store cubicles, and Roman villas with paintings still intact. Ghosts seemed to be watching us, ghosts of people just like us, whose lives had been snuffed out by volcanic ash and poison vapors. Gruesome plaster casts of some of the unfortunate victims had been preserved for viewing. Death had caught them unprepared. As our bodies cast lengthening shadows across the ground, I was reminded of the words of Job: "We are the sons of yesterday, we are but shadows."

I held Mike's hand tightly and wondered what he was thinking. I wondered if he thought that Pompeii might have been a part of his family's history. Mike's grandfather often spoke of growing up in the province of Avellino, the ancestral home of the Corcione family.

Before we had left for Italy, Mike's grandfather said to him, "Miguel, looka' for the volcano. When I wasa' a young man, I could see the volcano from my room."

We never did find grandpa's hometown. Avellino is a sprawling province of vineyards and rustic farmhouses. We wondered what drove both our ancestors to leave their native Europe and venture to America. What a miracle for Mike to return to the land of his ancestors—his life had come full circle.

The next day, we took a tour to the Isle of Capri, a high, rocky island that rose like the Tower of Babel into the blue Italian sky. We took a hydrofoil out to the island, where we were greeted by a small beach and colorful rowboats. The water was too rough for us to go to the Blue Grotto, but we enjoyed the little shops. The Blue Grotto promised pure turquoise water within the stillness of a reflective cave that could only be reached by a small boat when the tide was willing. I wish that someday I can return and experience the Blue Grotto.

To me, Rome was the most beautiful city on earth. I'll never forget Italy and the peace and beauty that surrounded me. The day we left, our eyes filled with tears. Together we sang "*Arriverderci Roma*" as the plane soared into the sky.

Mike and I had a spiritual awakening in that holy, ancient city. We returned to the trials of everyday life, dreaming of our vacation in Italy.

For the first time in our marriage, we were free to be ourselves. There was no one to impress, no one to apologize to for our parent's shortcomings, no one to put down our home, and no one to criticize my attempts at Italian cooking. In Rome, I learned to relax and love freely without abandon.

I wonder if our coins are still at the bottom of the Trevi Fountain. One night, soon after I returned, I dreamt that I returned to the Eternal City. The dream was so real and vivid that I felt my spirit had soared over the streets of Rome.

Today, I cherish the good memories and try to forget the bad ones. I struggle with catharsis of the soul. We returned to our mundane lives, Mike to driving his bread route, and me to struggling with the demands of marriage and motherhood. Most of the time, I wanted to leave, but I had nowhere to go. Maybe Mike felt the same! But I'll never forget those romantic nights under the canopy of stars, the late dinners in the dimly lit restaurant, and the marble suite in the palatial Roman hotel.

33

In 1977, we moved to a nice new home in Bayville. One day, Mike came home carrying a large apple pie. I looked at him suspiciously.

"Where did you get the pie?"

"My girlfriend made it for me."

"Looks delicious! Let's have a piece," I said with a smile.

It was. I waited for a chance to get even.

One day, I decided to make Mike his favorite dinner, lasagna. I made a big pan of lasagna and left it on the counter to cool. I cut a piece to test, but it was still a bit runny, so I decided to give it to the dog. I took out an old cereal bowl, put some canned dog food in the bottom, and put the lasagna on top. Our dog loved "people food," so I just left the food on the counter to cool.

Suddenly, Mike opened the front door and announced, "I'm home early. What's for dinner?"

"Lasagna," I said proudly, "it's cooling."

"Oh, yeah?"

"It has to set."

"Well, I'm hungry right now. What's this in this bowl? Looks good to me. Think I'll just help myself!"

"Go ahead, Mike."

He grabbed the bowl with the lasagna and dog food, sat down and ate the whole bowl.

"That was good," he exclaimed, wiping his mouth with a napkin, "and those meatballs were delicious!"

I never said a word.

Lori and Michael attended the local schools and seemed happy in their new environment. On summer days, they walked the horseshoe-shaped boardwalk that wound about the bay or swam in the warm waters of Barnegat Bay. Sometimes we sat beside the pier at Ocean Gate beach or splashed in the frigid red streams of Glen Cedars Park. My children made many new friends.

On a clear day, we could see, looking across Barnegat Bay to Seaside Heights, the outline of the log flume through the haze. Seaside Heights featured a long boardwalk complete with amusement rides, arcades, and barkers hawking everything from pizza to games of chance. The honky-tonk atmosphere reminded me of my old hometown of Asbury Park and how it used to be. There was always the beach and the bay for recreation. Once, the bay froze over and people raced iceboats or drove their cars over the ice.

My husband spent his Saturdays at Monmouth Park Racetrack, where the Corcione men held weekend reunions. Mike was a strong, healthy man, but he injured his back at work and began a downward spiral of disability. Little by little, he became disabled and couldn't work anymore.

34

On July 30, 1989, I received the phone call every parent dreads.

Michael was only twenty-one-years old. He was a vibrant, intelligent, handsome young man, almost six feet tall, and, like his father, a charmer with the ladies. Michael's dark black hair sometimes fell over his olive-skinned brow, highlighting his high cheekbones. He had graduated from Central Regional High School in Bayville, served in the Navy, and been a new-car salesman.

My son almost didn't pass this way again; it was a miracle that he survived the accident. The vehicle he was driving had flipped, throwing him forty feet along the edge of the Garden State Parkway. The staff at Southern Ocean County Hospital called to tell me that they would be airlifting him to Cooper Trauma Center, in Camden. The nurse told me that Michael could not feel his legs. I knew that Michael, my golden boy, may not survive, and if he did, he might never walk again.

When we first received the call, Mike grabbed his car keys and rushed toward the door. "You stay here," he warned, "you can't take it. "C'mon, Lori," he called, "let's go." Lori dropped what she was doing and raced down the stairs.

Thirty minutes later, Mike, sobbing, called me from Southern Ocean County Hospital: "Mike's hurt real bad, real bad. He's covered with blood and can't feel his legs. He may not make it . . .." His voice trailed off and he hung up.

My hands trembled as I held the phone. All the strength in my body left me. "My son, my son," I cried. The baby I had held in my arms, sang to, read poetry to, and cherished was critically injured. I couldn't even help him; paramedics were whisking him away by helicopter to be taken care of by strangers. I sank down on my knees and cried out to God for help.

My husband and daughter drove to Cooper Trauma Center that night, and I was left alone to face the uncertain night. All I could do was pray. I called my friend Cookie to pray with me. I called my priest, Father David. Somehow, I had faith that my son would survive. I called the hospital at all hours, inquiring about Michael, but there wasn't much hope. One of the nurses didn't think I heard her when she whispered to her co-worker, "What should I tell this woman? Her son's in bad shape . . .."

I don't know how I slept that night. I finally dozed off but awoke believing that I had simply experienced a terrible nightmare. I dreamt that my son had a terrible accident. I rubbed my eyes in disbelief, but as I looked around the empty house, I realized the nightmare was real. All was quiet. The July sun streamed through my window. There had been no call from the hospital. I jumped out of bed. Michael had made it through the night. There was hope. Immediately, I called the hospital again.

"Your son's condition is the same," said the trauma nurse on the other line.

I breathed a sigh of relief.

At that moment, I heard a car in the driveway, and in an instant, Mike and Lori came trudging up the stairs. My husband looked at me and said, "I have to get some rest, we'll go to the hospital later. Get ready."

He staggered into the bedroom and fell asleep on the bed.

Our priest called and said he would visit Michael in Cooper Trauma Center that afternoon. In August of 1989, Father David Vernak, my friends, and my congregation, would play an important part in restoring my family's faith during our time of trial. I remember throwing myself on the altar while sobbing and praying that my son survives his horrific accident.

When we arrived at the hospital later that afternoon, Father David was already there, reading his prayer book over our son. Michael was on a special trauma bed that rocked back and forth. His dark eyes flashed at me like a wounded animal. My husband and I were only allowed to stay for half an hour, but we could return later that afternoon for another visit.

Michael had made it through the first day; there *was* hope. We went home that night and hardly said a word. My husband was falling apart. I wondered if he blamed himself for the accident. He tried to make Michael a tough guy like himself, but Michael was even tougher than his father in his own way.

Michael made it through the second day, and on the third day, the doctors moved him to a step-down unit. Unfortunately, they never told us they were moving Michael, and when we entered the Trauma Unit, Michael's bed was empty. I reassured myself that perhaps the doctors had moved Michael, but my husband, on seeing the empty bed, fell to his knees and started sobbing. The nurses rushed toward us and reassured us that our son had been moved to a new unit.

It was August 2, 1989, my forty-fifth birthday. Michael had rallied against all odds. God was with him, and little by little, he grew stronger. Two months after entering the trauma center, he was transferred to Healthsouth Rehab. Though Michael was in a wheelchair, he went on to finish college on his own and live independently. A fantastic young man, he is an inspiration to us all. One of my son's favorite quotes is from Dylan Thomas: "Do not go gentle into that good night... rage, rage against the dying of the light."

Every day I thank God for saving my son's life and pray that someday Michael will walk again. Unfortunately, my husband suffered a nervous breakdown after our son's accident, and his health deteriorated.

Our dearest friend, Barry Slott, visited us and offered his help. Barry even came to our home and made pizza to cheer us up. Barry guided us with both Michael's and Mike's care and support. What would we have done without Barry? He was always there for us, lending a hand even in the darkest of days.

In 1994, my husband had a stroke and was admitted to a nursing home. I was forty-nine years old. Mike was fifty-two, but his handsome face had been altered forever. He looked as though he had been lobotomized. Even though his manliness and dignity had been assaulted, his face still held those green eyes, soft cheeks, and high Celtic brow. I stood by him and visited him almost every day of the eight years he was confined in the facility. Michael and Lori were heartbroken. I was heartbroken. His favorite uncles were shattered. I felt as though I had fallen down a flight of stairs. I was a backslider for a while, lost my faith, and ran away from reality, but gradually I dusted myself off and faced the situation.

During this time, my husband's old friends never forgot him. I realized the importance of friendship. Barry called every week and visited Mike often, offering support and advice. Richie and Roger King, Warren, and Johnny also called and visited. It was so reassuring to see that Mike's old friends had never forgotten him.

Years later, as I stared into my husband's vacant green eyes, I wondered if he remembered the good times—the good times when we were going together in high school, the good times in Italy, and the birth of our two children. His bright green eyes were dimmed, but he still managed to smile. Dementia was one of the saddest symptoms. I would ask myself: "Where *are* you, Mike; do you know who *I* am anymore? Do *I* know who I am anymore?"

I couldn't believe that my husband was a patient in a nursing home for eight years. How I hated him for his martyrdom, for being so strong when I was weak, for trying to control and dominate me. I wanted to shout at him: "I cannot heal you; I cannot help you, I cannot even take care of you anymore. I hate you for being sick, and I hate myself for standing here helplessly and watching you suffer."

Again, I turned to my books.

In *Resurrection,* Tolstoy states:

> We live in the belief that we are the masters of own lives and that they were given to us for our enjoyment. That is frankly absurd. If we have been sent into this world it is obviously by someone's will and *some* purpose. Yet we have assumed that we live only for our own selfish ends and inevitably things will go well for us. . ..

I became disillusioned about marriage and relationships and couldn't see myself ever getting seriously involved with another man. I just wanted to hide in my house and let life pass me by. In tragedy, my life had taken a new direction. I wanted to hide from life. I was living alone, running back and forth to the nursing home, helping my son, and dealing with the demands of social workers, and keeping up my house.

I identified with Ralph Ellison's statement that "he had been hurt to the point of invisibility."

Defeat fell on me like sleet. My son Michael came to my rescue.

"Why don't you finish your education, Mom? If I can do it, so can you! Here's the phone."

"OK, Michael, give me the phone."

My son challenged me to finish my education at Georgian Court College, a Catholic woman's college in Lakewood, NJ. I credit my son with my return to college, and my graduation. The classes were an inspiration for me. I was so impressed with the classes and curriculum that I even thought of going into a monastery. (My friends still laugh at this!)

I immersed myself in reading literature, studying, and meeting new friends. Georgian Court opened my eyes to a new sense of independence and confidence. I studied American and English literature, Shakespearean plays, and poetry. On my own, I was reading *The Fitzgeralds and the Kennedys,* by Doris Kearns Goodwin. I remember the passage when the maid said to the elderly Rose Kennedy, "Mrs. Kennedy, you had it all." Mrs. Kennedy replied curtly, "Yes, and I lost it all."

After I graduated, in 1995, I joined the Bayville book club and expanded my reading. None of my old friends could believe I belonged to a book club. I met wonderful friends at the book club: Jeanne, Alex, Ethel, and Irving. I felt that I was growing intellectually, but emotionally I was still very lonesome. Two of the first books we read were *The Remains of the Day* and *The Road from Coorain*. Some of my favorite literature tended toward the classics and biographies.

We had lively discussions about books, plays, local happenings, and ourselves. The book club was a form of therapy for me. Maybe it was therapy for all of us. I began to share my thoughts more openly than I had before. I was a "people pleaser" and tried to appear happy even though I sometimes didn't feel so upbeat. Sometimes I put on a smile even though I wasn't in a smiling mood. I was reaching out on my own to make a new life without my husband. It wasn't easy.

There were eight or ten regular members of the club. We met once a month, even in a blizzard! We read popular books and not-so-popular books. Surprisingly, some of us absolutely loved a book, and others absolutely hated it!

Sometimes the members laughed at my stories, and some members encouraged me to write a book about growing up in Asbury Park. My dear friend Jeanne gave me the confidence to put my thoughts and words on paper. When the group asked me to be chairman, I was surprised. Me, chairman of a book club? I was so proud of myself. I was a member for almost nine years, and the group meant a lot to me.

In the meantime, my neighbors reached out to me. I had lived in Bayville for twenty-two years, but I never really knew my neighbors. When my son was injured, my next-door neighbor, Yolie, sent me a lovely flower arrangement. Strangely enough, tragedy produced a new friend. Yolie reached out to me in my time of desperation. I didn't know Spanish people, so this was a new experience. I became friends with Yolie, her mother Ramona, and their little Chihuahua, Nanina. They invited me to their home for café and *arroz con frijoles colorados.*

With her dark hair, petite frame, and positive personality, Yolie personified my ideal of the Spanish culture. This friendship was a new and positive experience for me. Eventually, Yolie remarried and relocated to Cape Coral, Florida. I admire her—she had the guts to remarry and start her life all over again. We've been good friends for many years now, through thick and thin—mostly thin!

My neighbor Rose also befriended me. Rose was a gracious dark-haired woman who lived across the street from me. She used to stop and wave to me as she trimmed and manicured her lawn. I'll always remember her lush vegetable garden, delicate white-lace curtains, and the sweet taste of her fresh basil in my homemade tomato sauce. Rose and I took long walks together on the winding Ocean Gate boardwalk and let our problems drift away into the salty air. Rose was younger than me, but she became a widow before I did. Rose is gone now, but I'll never forget her strength and her wonderful laugh.

I discovered that I had to reach out to others; I needed companionship and moral support. It was time to heal old wounds and forgive my husband for his infidelities and egotism. In *The Cossacks,* Tolstoy states:

> The one way to be happy is to love, to love self-denyingly, to love every day and everything; to spread a web of love on all sides and to take all who come into it.

Soon the house needed major repairs. A leak in my son's downstairs bathroom almost caused the main beam under the house to collapse. The doors on the kitchen cabinets were falling apart, and mice scurried around the kitchen at night. I could hear the scruffy beasties clawing about the cabinets, scavenging for tasty morsels of food. One morning, I awoke and sleepily grabbed a piece of bread to pop in the toaster only to find a zapped mouse wedged inside the slot. Since then, I've been leery of toasters.

At night, I would listen for the furnace to kick in. Sometimes it would shudder and shut off in the middle of night. I prayed that the furnace would survive another winter. One night we had "thunder snow" and the heat ceased in the middle of a raging blizzard. I thought of my grandmother in winter and the mice skittering about her kitchen as the house grew cold as a stone.

Another time, I fell asleep to the sound of pouring rain, dreaming of a waterfall, only to wake up and see water pouring in through a hole in the roof. I ran outside in the pouring rain, found a garbage can, and put in under the leak.

I staggered my bills and haggled with bill collectors. My garden was a tangle of weeds. I thought of how Gran referred to herself as a "grass widow," a term that I never fully understood, though Gran said it meant a woman who was still married but alone. I thought of my mother; she, too, had been abandoned for so many years. I anguished over my future. What kind of disembodied family tradition had I inherited? I remembered reading Charles Dickens' *Bleak House,* an appropriate name for my home. I sat alone in my living room, facing the loss of my husband and my home.

It was difficult to realize that I had come so far since my children were born, only to face despair again. My thoughts strayed back to the time when I had no crib for my baby, only a dresser drawer. I remember washing my babies' diapers in the tub because I had no washing machine and discovering that my first house had a kerosene burner and a collapsed septic tank. No matter what, I learned to cook, and we always ate well, even if it was mostly Italian food. My father was so proud of me!

My mother, who had surprisingly recovered, extended a great deal of emotional support to me during my times of trial. Even though she had diabetes, she overcame the disease. My mother reassured me that I could face my problems and shoulder my responsibilities. Mother was downright heroic. She reminded me of her emotional breakdown and how she conquered the adversity of being poor. I listened to her voice of experience. I was grateful to God for healing my mother but saddened by the years she was sick. Sometimes I feel bitter, but I catch myself for my self-indulgence. I thank God for His healing power, since most schizophrenics never recover.

People ask me, "How did your mother get healed?" I always reply: "By the grace of God." There were no doctors, medicine, or therapy involved in my mother's recovery. If someone has a better answer, let them come forward. Only ten years before, people had signed a petition to hospitalize my mother again, and now she was well! Not only was she well again, but she was also happier and more confident than ever before, as if she was a young girl, full of life, promise, and good health. I had to get to know her again and love her again.

There is an inner beauty that emerges in one's victory over adversity. My mother grew more beautiful in her recovery. Her eyes were a brighter blue, her hair was blonder, and her smile more natural. Mother still looked tanned and beautiful and wore a new version of "Cyclamen Evening," the bright pink lipstick she always loved.

The older I get, the more I miss my mother.

I had to learn to forgive my mother and accept the fact that her behavior was due to a vicious, unpredictable illness. I also had to learn to forgive my father. In his anger, he turned me against my mother for many years. I must admit that I loved my mother and admired her for overcoming her schizophrenia, nervous breakdown, agoraphobia, and diabetes. In the end, my mother emerged as a strong woman.

I was openly proud of my mother. She loved my two children and showered them with gifts and attention. My children had a new grandmother. In her recovery, my mother recaptured her devotion to her family. We had family dinners together, complete with all my mother's homemade pies and pastries. The family was together again. My mother went back to work in her beloved candy store. This would have been impossible years before. It was reassuring how the customers welcomed her back, many of them remembering her when she was young. Her skin had regained its glow, and her eyes sparkled like the sea on a summer morning.

Watching my mother's recovery was like watching a miracle unfold. She had made a complete turnaround. My mother and I reconciled when I was in my thirties. We would spend many quiet times together, sitting on the beach, swimming in the ocean, and browsing for antiques along the streets of Ocean Grove. Sometimes we'd stroll over to Day's Ice Cream Parlor and eat strawberry ice cream cones.

We would sit together on Loch Arbour Beach, laugh, and share memories of the good times, when we were all much younger. Amazing as it sounds, it was as though nothing ever happened. The nor'easter had torn apart our lives. Now, the sea was calm again.

Once, on the way to the beach, we saw a sign outside our local restaurant that read "Lobster Dinner- $9.99." What a bargain! As we sat on the beach, we wished we could afford that lobster dinner, but abandoned all hope. Oh well, all we could do was take a dip in the ocean, so we waded into the cold water. The waves came, so we headed for shore, and as my mother neared the piling, she tugged on the rope to guide her. Lo and behold, as the rope came out of the water, there was a $20 bill wrapped around it!

On the way home we stopped at the restaurant and enjoyed our steamed lobster dinners together.

One day we decided to drive by Gran's house, the family homestead at 4 Atlantic Avenue, Bradley Beach, just a few blocks from the beach. We hadn't been there in a long while, and when we drove by, we didn't recognize the house. We stopped short and thought we were dreaming! The rickety porch and clapboard exterior had been replaced by bright white vinyl siding, a modern garage, and entranceway. By coincidence, Gran's favorite red geraniums still sat faithfully beside her white wicker sofa, the same wicker set where we used to sit together many summer evenings years ago.

My mother and I knocked on the door. A gracious, smiling, woman answered the door almost as if she were expecting us. We explained that this had been our family's home. The new owner graciously invited us in and gave us a tour of what was once Gran's old home. My mother told of how her father had built the home in the 1900s. We couldn't believe our eyes when we saw the beautiful new living room, parlor, and kitchen! Our host took us upstairs to the remodeled bedrooms. My old bedroom faced east. I remember reading by the glassy green dragonfly Tiffany lamp and falling asleep listening to the sounds of the sea. The rickety stairs were gone, but the claw-foot tub was still there. The entire house was a showplace—bright and colorful.

If only Gran could have seen the transformation of her Queen Anne Home! She would have been so proud. So were we! We thanked the new owner for her hospitality and all her hard work. Everything had come full circle. Gran lived a long healthy life, going home to the Lord at age ninety-four and living long enough to see her daughter's return to sanity.

I honestly believe God gave me back my mother. One of the most noticeable changes I noticed was that Mother had developed a lively sense of humor. After my daughter got divorced, I told my mother that Lori was seeing a young man named Dwayne.

My mother just turned to me and smiled, "Well, I guess all the money you spent on Lori's wedding went down the Dwayne!"

35

During this time, God also gave me a new companion. His name was Bill, and his wife was in the same nursing home as my husband. I guess Bill and I both needed someone to talk to. In fact, our families encouraged us to get together. (Maybe we were getting on their nerves!)

Bill invited me to go for dinner at Charlie Brown's with his two cousins, Marge and Doris. It had to be on a Wednesday night, when Charlie Brown's served free shrimp cocktail with dinner. We had a relaxing dinner, and Bill and I have been together ever since. Must have been the shrimp.

Finally, we had someone to share our problems with. We loved our spouses, but it had become a lonesome life for both of us, and now we could discuss our concerns with someone who was going through the same experience. All we could do was watch our loved ones fade away, while we stood helplessly by. This is a frustrating experience, just watching.

In the winter, we went dancing at Ocean Acres Country Club, and in the summer, we enjoyed boating at Berkeley Island, Bayville. And we both visited our spouses faithfully.

This was the life I never had with my husband—dining, dancing, and boating. Bill took Lori, Michael, and me for a ride on his new twenty-three-foot cabin cruiser, *Blue Champagne*. We enjoyed a brilliant summer day on the bay, and at the end, we wolfed down burgers and fries at our favorite restaurant in Ocean Gate, the Anchor Inn.

I was shocked to discover that Bill was twenty-four years older than me. He seemed so vibrant and positive about life. I was really drawn to him because I feared getting old and being alone, but he assured me that older people sometimes are happier and more vibrant than younger people. What really intrigued me was that Bill was a successful, hardworking man who also had plain *good luck*. He had a good marriage, nice personality, and two successful careers. Besides serving in World War II, he graduated from the Merchant Marine Academy when he was fifty years old. He also sailed up the Mississippi as first mate on the tanker, *The Jamie Baxter*. Bill had come into my life unexpectedly, and I liked keeping company with this gentleman.

Mike passed away on June 22, 2002, after his long, debilitating illness, and his eight-year confinement in a nursing home. Mike's old friends never forgot him—Roger King came to the wake, as did Henry Vaccaro and Carl Williams. Roger, Richie, and Michael King helped pay for my husband's funeral. At the memorial, Mike's longtime friends, Barry and Warren, gave loving testimonies to their friend.

In 2004, I sold my home in Bayville and moved to Florida with Bill. Coincidentally, I found a little Orthodox church across the street from Bill's house, where I could pray and find peace. Leaving the Jersey Shore was heart-wrenching, but I wanted to make a new life for myself and leave the bad memories behind. I met new friends and made new memories.

At times, the past lingered in the far shadows of my mind, but after all my trials and traumatic events, I stopped questioning my sanity. The beast that lurked in the shadows was gone. We may never know what circumstances or genetic components cause madness. Doctors and psychiatrists promote theories, but they don't offer a conclusive cure. Modern medicine has created asylums without walls.

I never could accept my mother's illness until I accepted the truth. My mother's madness is a part of me. Madness can strike anyone—it is no respecter of persons. The day the paramedics came to take my mother away was the day we were linked forever in the battle for sanity.

Part of the insanity of life is called marriage. Both men and women build their hopes on marriage, hoping they will create a successful marriage. I tried hard to achieve this Utopia. My children, home, and family meant the world to me. I navigated through storms of poverty, infidelity, illness, and accidents. Marriage created and destroyed my mother, and marriage created and destroyed me. Like my mother, I have my own faults. I have met my own demons. I have fallen down many times, but each time I managed to get up again.

Michael graduated college and went on to work in the stock market and sales fields. He has traveled to Europe and lives in Florida. Lori is happily married to her husband, Lenny. Both own their own homes and live independently. I'm very proud of my children and their accomplishments.

I thank God that my mother recovered. I have fond memories of sitting together on the beach, watching the sun sparkle on the sea. I smile when I remember the $20 bill she found in the ocean that bought us a lobster dinner. My mother reunited the family and brought us together for special holiday dinners, complete with roast lamb on Easter and roast turkey on Christmas. I sat there in amazement as I watched my father take his rightful place at the head of the table. His bitterness disappeared, redeeming him as a wonderful, caring man who loved his family.

My mother had forgiven my father and admitted that she still loved him. I guess she loved us all. She cried when my father died on Christmas Day, her birthday.

I remember sitting next to my mother at Lori's wedding and thinking how beautiful my mother and daughter looked. I remember Ocean Grove, as my mother and I scoured the quaint shops for antiques, stopping only for ice cream at the old-fashioned ice cream parlor. I remember how she loved my family unconditionally.

One of the strangest things happened after my mother recovered. All those years when my mother was sick, the house had fallen into neglect. Mother often joked that if she had only fifty thousand dollars, she could fix up the house like it used to be. We all laughed—we knew that it was impossible. About a year later, Mother received a certified letter informing her that Uncle Fred had passed away and left my mother fifty thousand dollars! The entire family was stunned.

After reading the letter aloud to me, she turned to me and said: "You see, I told you so! God answered my prayers!"

She fixed up the house.

On the morning of August 28, 2008, my mother passed away after a brief illness. Her life had ended. She was eighty-six. Bill and I had planned a trip to New Jersey on September 1; we missed my mother's passing by a few days.

I dreaded the visit, visualizing the scene in *Gone with the Wind*, when Scarlet O'Hara returned to Tara only to find her house in ruins and her mother dead.

Publicly I put up a good front, but privately I cried bitter tears, tears of anger and of sorrow. I could never take her place. I will always remember my mother as a beautiful, refined, and intelligent woman who overcame mental illness, divorce, and diabetes. She even outlived her doctors. During the last years of her life, my brother Phil was her caregiver.

I wonder if I failed her as a daughter. Yet, I am proud that I gave my mother her first two grandchildren. Sometimes I look into my daughter's green eyes and see both my mother and my husband's mother. I am thankful to God for my blessings, but I anguish over the lost years. I miss my mother today and still feel that a part of me is gone. It's as though my life was blazing like a log burning in a fireplace when suddenly a section of the log breaks off and is consumed in the flames, to be lost forever.

36

Bill and I drove up from Florida to attend my mother's funeral. The wake was packed with family and friends.

Mother's old friends from the Greek community came to see Mother for the last time. Even though she wasn't Greek, the Greek community of Asbury Park had always accepted her as one of their own. Her elegant friend, Lorraine Newman, came to me and hugged me tightly. Smiling, she reminded me of how much she loved my mother. My father's brother, Uncle Tutti, paid his final respects. My old friend Nancy was there.

Lori and Lenny, her husband, wept openly. Michael had tears in his eyes. I cleared my throat and read my eulogy:

> *My mother was the classic beauty; not only was she beautiful, she had class too. Mother was born in Ocean Grove and grew up in Bradley Beach. Mother was born on Christmas and my grandmother always said, 'Mother was her Christmas gift.'*
>
> *Mother loved the Jersey Shore and proclaimed it the 'most beautiful place on earth.' My mother was Dutch and English. The family overcame poverty and adversity*

of growing up without a father and persevered toward success.

I remember my mother telling me about the day she met my father. Mother was walking along Cookman Avenue, Asbury Park, with her friend Eileen. My mother turned to Eileen and announced: "I think I'll go into this candy store and ask for a job." Not only did my mother get the job, she also married the proprietor. During the Second World War, my mother helped run the candy store while my father was away in the Navy. She took care of the house and the business, and even had her first baby.

Mother proved to everyone that she was not just another pretty face, but a woman of depth, integrity, and generosity. She had a good business mind, too, and expanded the Caramel Shop Candies to our second store, on Highway 35. How my mother loved that candy store! She loved the red-satin hearts of Valentine's Day, the chocolate bunnies of Easter, and the salt-water taffy of summer. Most of all, Mother loved the customers. She always greeted them warmly and called them by name. Mother reached out to the Greek community and made wonderful friends with the good Greeks of Asbury Park. She adopted the Greek faith and learned to make kourambiedes and baklava.

My mother was a very positive person; during my time of troubles, she encouraged me to remain strong. When I remember my mother, I remember how she loved her home, her family, and the peaceful town of Interlaken.

One of my mother's favorite songs was "The Green, Green Grass of Home." Sometimes she would sing the refrain aloud, saying that the lyrics reminded her of 411 Windermere. Most of all, my mother loved the sea. In my mind, I can still picture her laughing and smiling, holding hands with her friends—bathing beauties, as they emerge from the sea. Somewhere, at this very moment, her spirit is floating free from the bonds of this earth. I can picture her splashing in the sea—young and beautiful again.

I hardly finished the eulogy before I began to choke up.

Mother, I love you.

Lori was weeping, but she helped me sit down. Well, it's finished, I thought to myself. My mother's life has found closure. I know her soul is at peace.

Perhaps, somewhere in a parallel universe, my family and I are all together again. In reality, I live alone in my lovely new home, listening to the wind whining through the Spanish moss. I wonder what twist of fate led me to the west coast of Florida and the rural hamlet called Masaryktown.

It's midnight and I'm sleepy. I miss my family, but remind myself of how blessed I am. The past will always be lurking in the shadows, waiting to sneak up and grab me. The future is uncertain, so I guess I'll just have to live one day at a time. I toss and turn, thinking of my grandmother, my mother, and me, while reflecting on the difficulties of fulfilling the roles of wife, mother, and daughter.

I reflect on the photo of the three of us as we sat on my mother's front steps when I was a baby. I was the first of a new generation, a child of promise. I picture my aristocratic grandmother holding her head high as my mother held me on her lap, beaming proudly.

I try to sleep, but just outside my window a lonely owl, huddling in the arms of the majestic oaks, hoots in the darkness. I throw the covers aside and peer through the window. I can't see the owl, a phantom in the shadows, but I know he's there. His call floats on the wind. Somewhere, off in the distance, the plaintive whistle of a train pierces the silence as it lumbers through the lonely night.

I remember when I was a young girl, and how the whistle of the owl train roused me from my sleep, threatening to steal my soul. Now I just pull the covers over my head and go back to sleep. I'm no longer afraid of losing my soul. I just turn over, say my prayers, and give my problems to God. Then I'll sleep well, and my head will be full of dreams—good dreams.

Gran, Marjorie, and baby Joanie

Joan Marie Corcione (1944-2018) was born and raised on the Jersey Shore. She graduated *magna cum laude* from Georgian Court University, raised two children, and worked as a teacher. A painter and poet, Joan was loved dearly.

Made in the USA
Columbia, SC
06 July 2023

19647334R00153